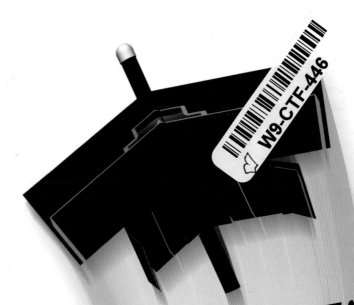

STRAW SHOOTER

JETS

by the editors of Klutz

KLUTZ®

KLUTZ®

creates activity books and other great stuff for kids ages 3 to 103. We began our corporate life in 1977 in a garage we shared with a Chevrolet Impala. Although we've outgrown that first office, Klutz galactic headquarters is still staffed entirely by real human beings. For those of you who collect mission statements, here's ours:

• Create wonderful things • Be good • Have fun

Write Us

We would love to hear your comments regarding this or any of our books. We have many!

KLUTZ®

557 Broadway
New York, NY 10012
thefolks@klutz.com

Distributed in the UK
by Scholastic UK Ltd
Westfield Road
Southam, Warwickshire
England CV47 0RA

Distributed in Canada
by Scholastic Canada Ltd
604 King Street West
Toronto, Ontario
Canada M5V 1E1

Distributed in Australia
by Scholastic Australia Ltd
PO Box 579
Gosford, NSW
Australia 2250

Distributed in Hong Kong
by Scholastic Hong Kong Ltd
Suites 2001-2, Top Glory Tower
262 Gloucester Road
Causeway Bay, Hong Kong

Manufactured in China. 73

ISBN 978-0-545-64779-3

4 1 5 8 5 7 0 8 8

HOW TO BUILD EACH STRAW SHOOTER JET

EQUIPMENT CHECKLIST

The paper airplanes you're used to are mere gliders. You launch them with brute force, and they're big enough to compensate for a sloppy or inaccurate throw.

But the micro-planes in this book are sleek, precise instruments, which call for something more advanced: **Jet propulsion**.

What turns a plane into a jet? Compressed air power. The brightly colored plastic tubes in this book are no ordinary drinking straws. They are high-precision air compression chambers. All they need is your lung power.

Are YOU a windbag? Perfect — you can be a pilot.

To start building your fleet, you'll need:

STUFF YOU HAVE ALREADY

scissors

tape

THE STUFF THAT COMES WITH THIS BOOK

4 launch straws

10 jet straws

10 nose cones

THE FLEET SHEETS!

The last 30 leaves of the book are what we call the "Fleet Sheets." This is where you'll find all five different Straw Shooter Jets, two on each sheet. If you do the math, that's 60 jets. Don't tear them out. We'll show you how to cut out the jets one at a time.

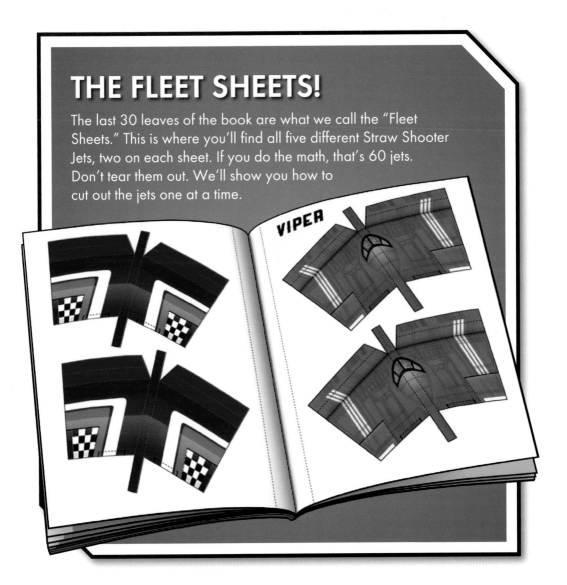

Each jet comes in five different graphic styles.

Behind the fleet sheets is a

STENCIL.

Use it to make jets in your own style.

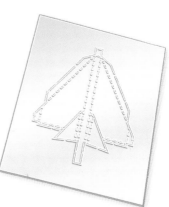

Before you make your first jet, read these tips.

GETTING JET SET

CUTTING

1 STAY LOOSE

Remove the jet you need from the fleet sheet with a LOOSE cut. It will make the smaller, detailed cuts easier.

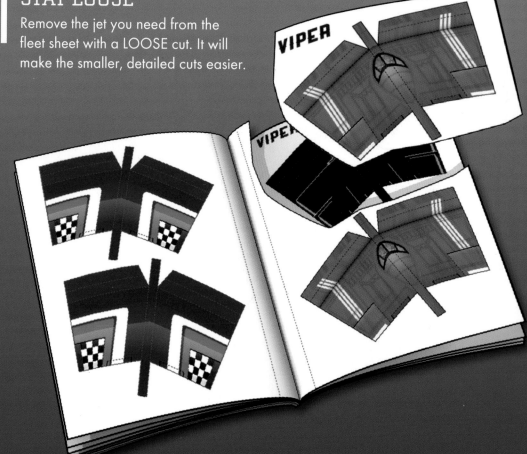

2 OUTLINE CUT

After the jet is loosely cut from the fleet sheet page, cut around the outline.

To cut clean angles, first cut along one side (A), and then move back to the outer edge and cut along another (B).

Have the cuts meet in the corner.

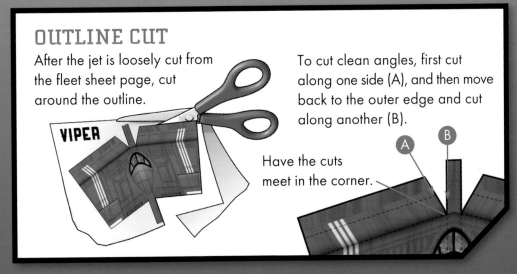

A

B

VIPER

3 DETAILED CUTS

Cut stops here

Solid black lines are cut lines.

Dotted black lines are fold lines.

Cut line

Fold line (do not cut)

Cut lines

FOLDING

Make your folds crisp by running your finger or fingernail along them, pressing the paper nice and flat.

Look at the pictures as you go. Check often to make sure your plane looks just like the picture. If it doesn't, go back a few steps.

To make a jet that flies well, fold exactly on the dotted lines. If you're finding any folds tricky to do, try these expert strategies.

Find something flat and straight-edged, like a playing card. Set the straight edge along the dotted line and fold the paper over it.

Pinch the fold at each end of the dotted line. Then flatten between the ends to finish the fold.

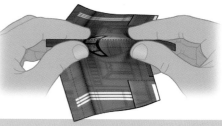

Or, just rotate the paper and try again. Sometimes it helps to approach a problem from a different angle.

TAPING

The last step of assembly uses tape. Here are some taping tips.

Make taping easier by tearing a few small pieces, about ½ inch (1 cm) long, and sticking them along a table edge. That way you have a ready supply when needed.

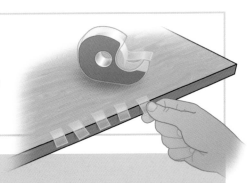

KEEP IT LIGHT.
Don't overdo the tape. Each piece adds some weight to your plane. Use only the amount of tape described in the instructions.

STAY EVEN.
Keep your tape symmetrical — if you add tape on one wing, add a piece of tape of the same size on the other wing.

Sometimes you'll need skinny strips of tape. Make them by vertically tearing a regular piece of tape in two.

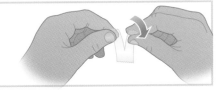

FLIGHT SCHOOL

WITH STRAW SHOOTER JET MASTER PILOT — P. SHOOTER

Take it from me, it takes more than a pair of wings to make a straw fly. To be an ace pilot, you've got to go to school.

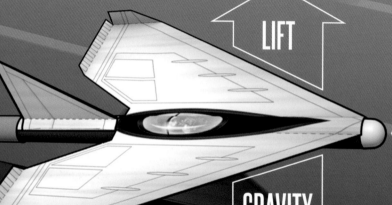

LIFT

DRAG

GRAVITY

BASIC TRAINING

When your jet flies through the air, **GRAVITY** pulls it downward. At the same time, air flowing around your jet pushes it upward, a force called **LIFT**. And the effort of pushing air aside slows your jet down, a force called **DRAG**.

FLYING RIGHT

To change how your jet flies, adjust its flaps, fins, and wings. By bending these surfaces, you change how air flowing over the jet pushes against it — and that can make the jet climb, crash, or do cool stunts.

FLAPS ON THE WINGS

- Both flaps up — jet climbs
- Both flaps down — jet dives
- Left up; right down — left turn
- Right up; left down — right turn

Raised flaps send the air up, which pushes the back of the jet down. When the back goes down, the nose tilts up — and the jet climbs.

WINGS

- These jets fly best when the wings form a wide V shape
- The angle of the wings is called the dihedral angle or just plain dihedral

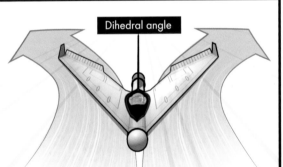

Dihedral angle

Check for symmetry — your jet's left half should match the right.

VERTICAL STABILIZERS

- Tail fins keep the jet's rear in line with the nose
- Winglets and tail fins keep the flight straight and steady

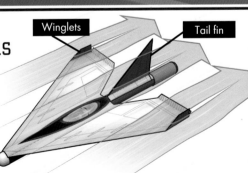

Winglets

Tail fin

If tail fins and winglets are crooked, they won't do their job.

YOUR JET IS ASSEMBLED? IT'S TIME FOR LAUNCH.

ON YOUR STRAW,

GET SET,

Angle the straw upward.

BLOW!

GET RAD!

It's all about getting R.A.D., better known as RAPID AIR DEPLOYMENT

1. Take a deep breath and stick the straw in your mouth.
2. Block the end of the straw with your tongue.
3. To launch, quickly move your tongue to unblock the straw and blast the jet off with a sudden burst of air.

If you did it right, you'll hear a satisfying "POP" as the jet launches.

Make sure you are launching your jets in a clear area. And never shoot your jets at anyone. Got it? Good.

DRAGONFLY

A natural glider, the Dragonfly can soar for extreme distances with hardly any effort. Because the wing is set high above the fuselage, or body, the Dragonfly has a steady flight that even a rookie can handle.

HIGH WING

FUSELAGE

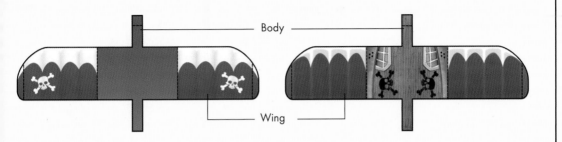

TOP SIDE

UNDERSIDE

Body

Wing

CUT OUT THE DRAGONFLY

For cutting tips, see page 7

FOLDING

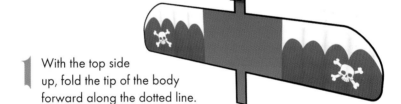

1 With the top side up, fold the tip of the body forward along the dotted line.

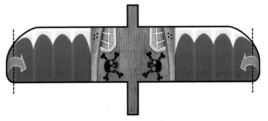

2 Flip the jet over and fold the end of each wing in along the dotted lines as shown. These will be the winglets.

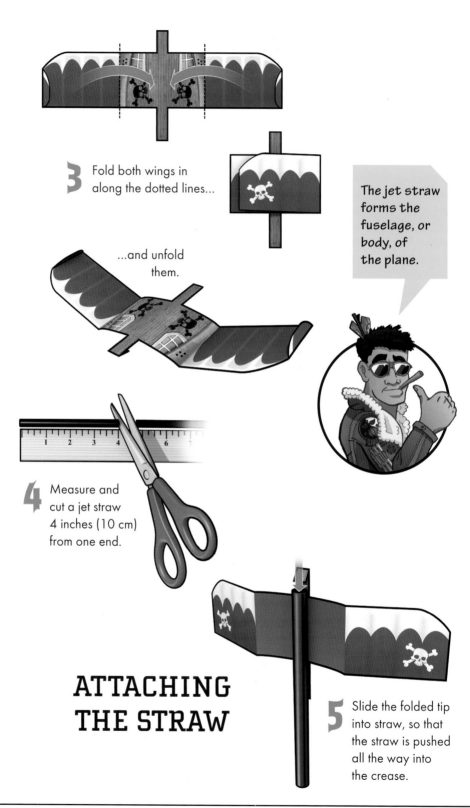

3 Fold both wings in along the dotted lines...

...and unfold them.

The jet straw forms the fuselage, or body, of the plane.

This is 4 inches.

4 Measure and cut a jet straw 4 inches (10 cm) from one end.

ATTACHING THE STRAW

5 Slide the folded tip into straw, so that the straw is pushed all the way into the crease.

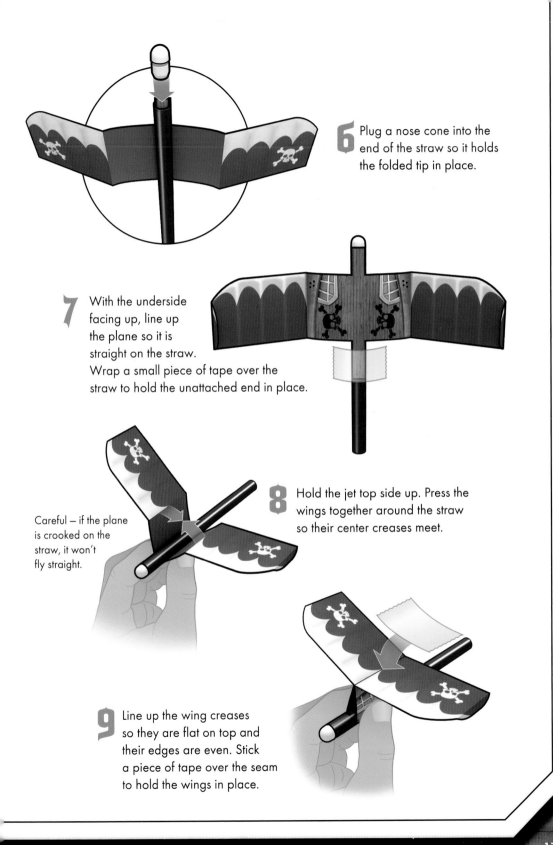

6 Plug a nose cone into the end of the straw so it holds the folded tip in place.

7 With the underside facing up, line up the plane so it is straight on the straw. Wrap a small piece of tape over the straw to hold the unattached end in place.

Careful – if the plane is crooked on the straw, it won't fly straight.

8 Hold the jet top side up. Press the wings together around the straw so their center creases meet.

9 Line up the wing creases so they are flat on top and their edges are even. Stick a piece of tape over the seam to hold the wings in place.

FLIGHT CHECK

Look at your jet from above. Make sure all three lines marked here are straight and line up with the straw. If they don't, fix them.

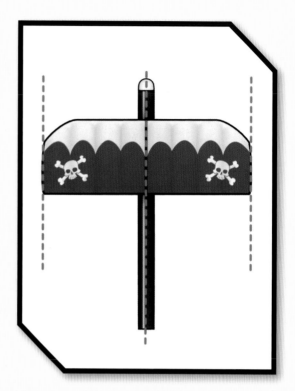

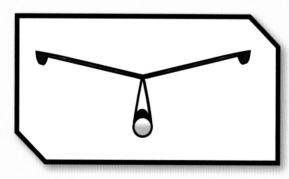

BALANCE

Then look at your jet from the back. The wings should be symmetrical (looking the same on both sides) and form a shallow V shape. Does your jet match the picture? If not, adjust it.

READY FOR A TEST FLIGHT!

DRAGONFLY
REAL AIRCRAFT INSPIRATION

HANG GLIDER

A hang glider has no engine. It relies on rising currents of warm air to stay aloft. Like the Dragonfly, a hang glider's wings are located high above the heaviest point of the aircraft. Since it has no flaps, the pilot must shift the weight of his or her body to steer. This aircraft is light enough for a person to carry, yet a skilled pilot can simply walk off a cliff and soar hundreds of miles.

STRAWHAWK

PERFORMANCE

SPEED	/▮▮▮▮▮▮▮	
RANGE	/▮▮▮	
AGILITY	/▮▮▮▮▮▮▮	
CONTROL	/▮▮▮▮	
STYLE	/▮▮▮▮▮▮	

The trapezoid wing shape of the Strawhawk is perfect for high speed and combat superiority. Its unconventional V tail makes the plane lighter, but more challenging to control. With a higher speed but a shorter range, the Strawhawk is more like a dart than a glider.

TRAPEZOID WING

V-TAIL

TOP SIDE

UNDERSIDE

Wing

Tail

Body

Be sure to make
the detailed cuts.

CUT OUT THE STRAWHAWK
For cutting tips, see page 7

FOLDING

1 With the underside facing
up, fold down along the
diagonal dotted lines
on each wing.

2 Stick a piece of tape on each
wing to hold the folds in place.
Match the size and placement
of the tape on each wing as
closely as you can.

3 Flip the jet top side up and fold the wing tips in along the dotted lines. These will be the winglets.

4 Fold the left wing and tail in. Crease, and then unfold.

5 Do the same with the right wing and tail fin — fold, crease, and unfold.

6 Fold the flap on each wing up along the dotted line. Crease, and then unfold. These will be the flaps.

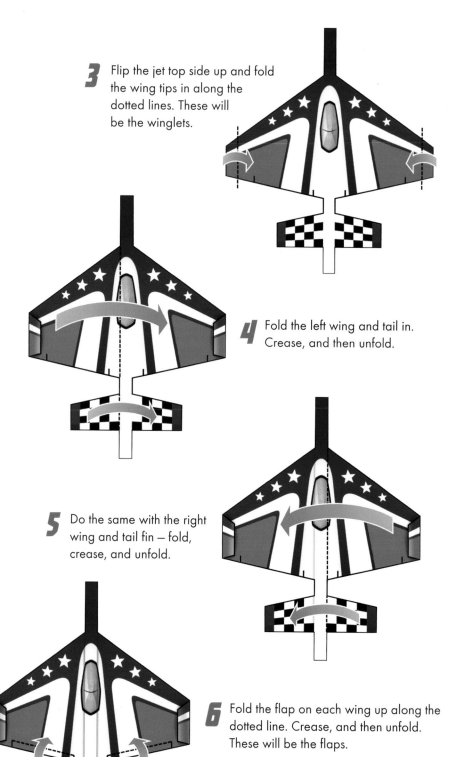

ATTACHING THE STRAW

7 Flip the jet underside up. Fold the tip of the body down along the dotted line.

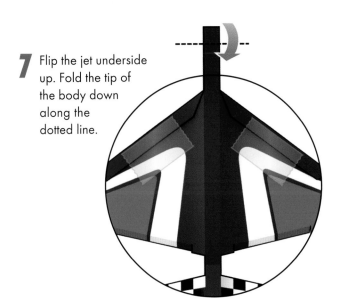

Does your plane look just like the picture? Check it now. If it doesn't, go back a few steps.

8 Slide the folded tip into a full-length straw, so that the straw is pushed all the way into the crease.

Plug the straw with a nose cone to hold the folded tip in place.

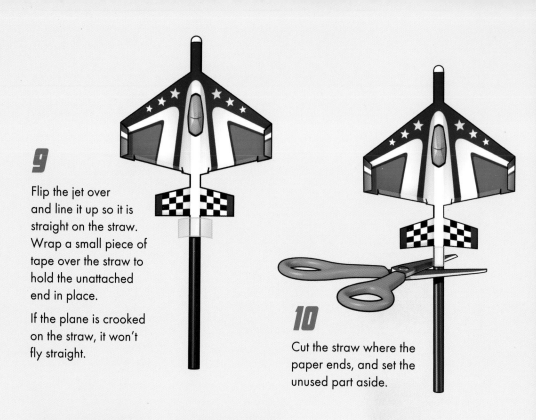

9

Flip the jet over and line it up so it is straight on the straw. Wrap a small piece of tape over the straw to hold the unattached end in place.

If the plane is crooked on the straw, it won't fly straight.

10

Cut the straw where the paper ends, and set the unused part aside.

FLIGHT CHECK

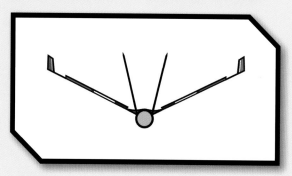

BALANCE

Look at your jet from the back. The wings should be symmetrical (looking the same on both sides) and form a shallow V shape. The tail fins should be nearly vertical. Does your jet match the picture? If not, adjust it.

READY FOR A TEST FLIGHT!

STRAWHAWK

REAL AIRCRAFT INSPIRATION

F-22 RAPTOR

The F-22 Raptor is the most advanced US fighter jet. Its ultra-modern shape inspired the Strawhawk's delta wing and V tail. The Raptor's stealth technology is so powerful that when it flies by, radar systems detect an object only the size of a Strawhawk.

VIPER

SPEED	▰▰▰	
RANGE	▰▰▰▰▰▰▰	
AGILITY	▰▰▰	
CONTROL	▰▰▰	
STYLE	▰▰▰▰▰	

The Viper is a broad-winged glider with a "flying wing" design, which means that most of the aircraft is one big wing. This gives it very low drag. What it gains in low drag, it loses in stability. A true flying wing would have no tail, but the Viper's twin tail keeps it more stable at low speeds.

TWIN TAIL

FLYING WING

TOP SIDE

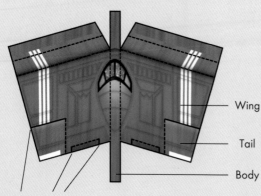

Be sure to make
the detailed cuts.

UNDERSIDE

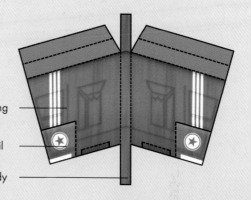

Wing

Tail

Body

CUT OUT THE VIPER
For cutting tips, see page 7

FOLDING

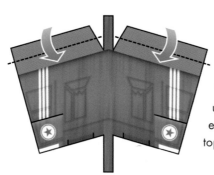

1

With the underside facing
up, fold the front edge of
each wing down along the
top dotted line...

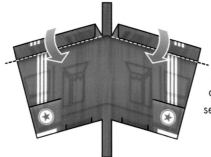

...and fold them
again along the
second dotted line.

2 Stick a piece of tape on each wing to hold the folds in place. Match the size and placement of the tape on each wing as closely as you can.

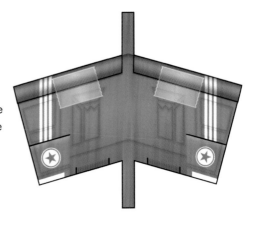

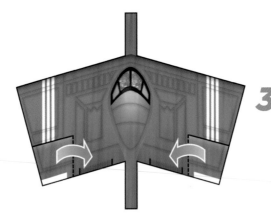

3 Flip the plane top side up and fold the big flaps in along the dotted lines. Crease, then unfold. These will be the jet's tail fins.

4 Fold the left wing and tail in. Crease, and then unfold.

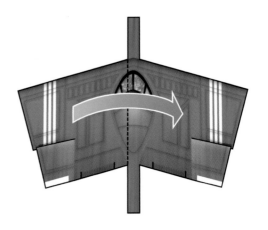

5 Do the same with the right wing and tail — fold, crease, and unfold.

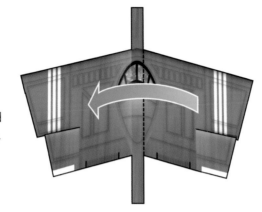

6 Now fold the tiny flaps on each wing up along the dotted line. Crease, and then unfold.

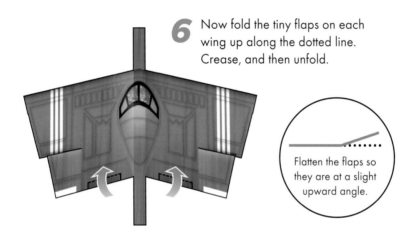

Flatten the flaps so they are at a slight upward angle.

7 Flip the jet underside up. Fold the tip of the body down along the dotted line.

ATTACHING THE STRAW

8 Slide the folded tip into a full-length straw, so that the straw is pushed all the way into the crease...

Pay attention! The most important part of any aircraft is between the pilot's ears. If your head's already in the clouds, the rest of you will never get there.

...then plug the straw with a nose cone to hold the folded tip in place.

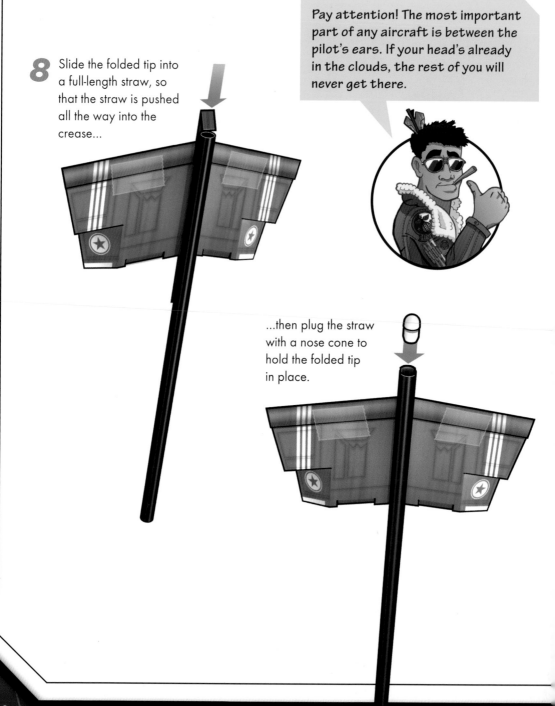

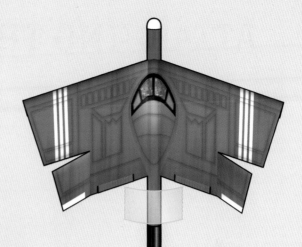

9 Flip the jet over and line it up so it is straight on the straw. Wrap a small piece of tape over the straw to hold the unattached end in place.

If the plane is crooked on the straw, it won't fly straight.

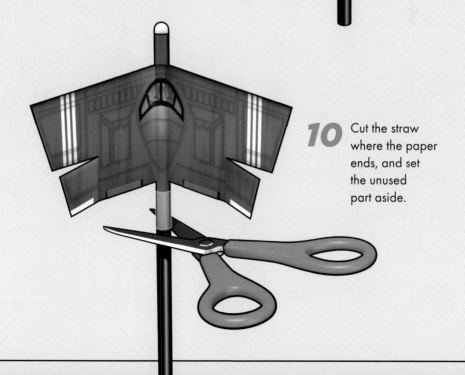

10 Cut the straw where the paper ends, and set the unused part aside.

FLIGHT CHECK

Make sure the flaps are at a slight upward angle, and all the other folds are straight and line up with the straw. If they don't, fix them.

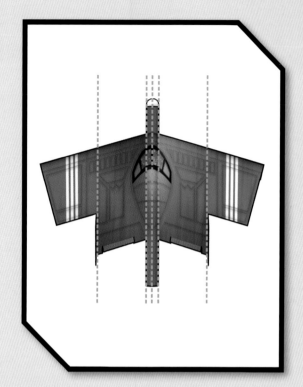

BALANCE

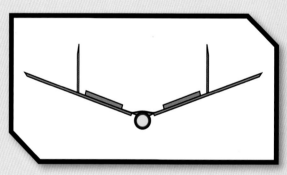

Look at your jet from the back. The wings should be symmetrical (looking the same on both sides) and form a shallow V-shape. The tail fins should be vertical. Does your jet match the picture? If not, adjust it.

READY FOR A TEST FLIGHT!

VIPER
REAL AIRCRAFT INSPIRATION

B-2 SPIRIT

We modeled the Viper's cockpit, flying wing design, and jagged silhouette on the B-2 Spirit. Unlike the Viper, the B-2 has no tail or fuselage at all, making it a true flying wing. It can fly more than 6,000 miles before refueling in midair. Because each plane costs over $2 billion to manufacture, there are only 21 of them in the world.

X-88

SPEED	▮▮▮▮▯
RANGE	▮▮▮▮▮
AGILITY	▮▮▮▯▯
CONTROL	▮▮▮▮▮
STYLE	▮▮▮▮▮▮

The X-88 is proof that a jet doesn't need to be "airplane-shaped" to fly well. This jet has tandem box wings: "Tandem" means one wing is behind the other. "Box" means the wings are joined at the tips. With two wings, it has twice the lift, so it takes only a little power to fly long distances.

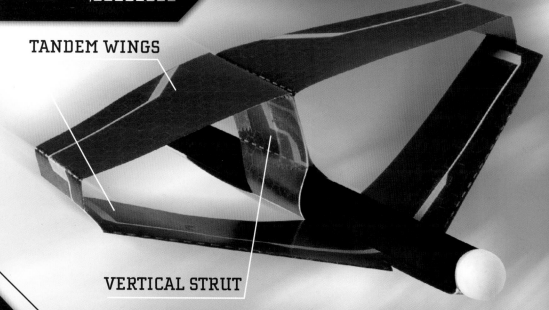

TANDEM WINGS

VERTICAL STRUT

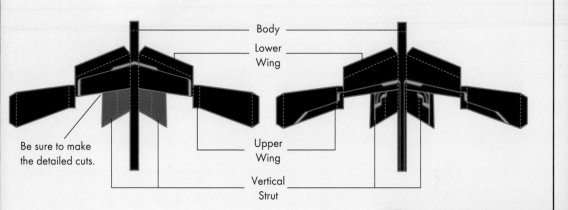

TOP SIDE

UNDERSIDE

Body

Lower
Wing

Be sure to make
the detailed cuts.

Upper
Wing

Vertical
Strut

CUT OUT THE X·88
For cutting tips, see page 7

FOLDING

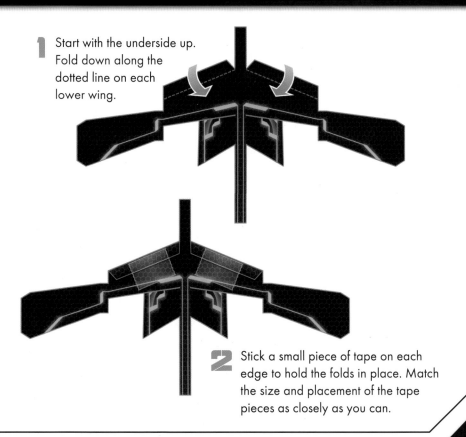

1 Start with the underside up.
Fold down along the
dotted line on each
lower wing.

2 Stick a small piece of tape on each
edge to hold the folds in place. Match
the size and placement of the tape
pieces as closely as you can.

3 Flip the jet over. Now fold in, crease, and unfold one wing along the three dotted lines. Do the same with the other wing.

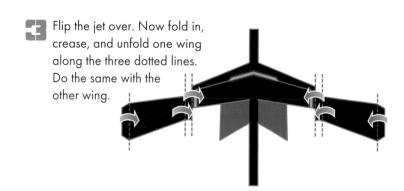

4 Fold the left side of the vertical strut in along the dotted line.

Then fold the same side back along the dotted line that is printed on the underside. Crease and unfold both folds.

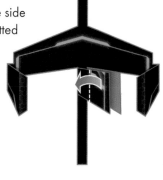

5 Repeat step 4 with the right side of the vertical strut.

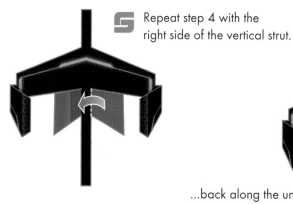

...back along the underside dotted line, and then unfold.

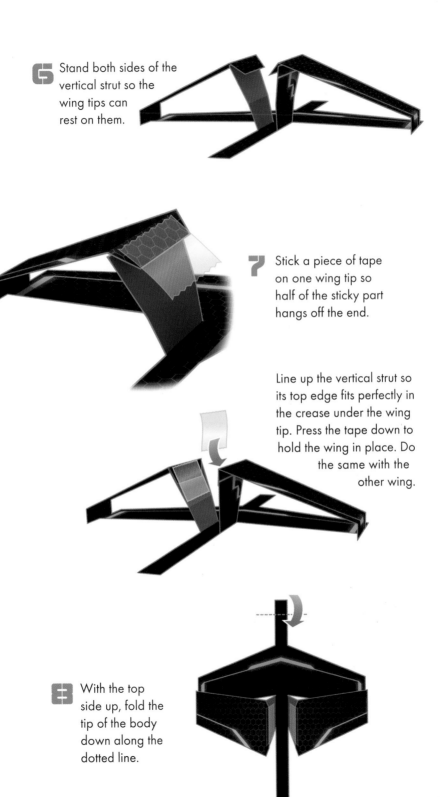

6 Stand both sides of the vertical strut so the wing tips can rest on them.

7 Stick a piece of tape on one wing tip so half of the sticky part hangs off the end.

Line up the vertical strut so its top edge fits perfectly in the crease under the wing tip. Press the tape down to hold the wing in place. Do the same with the other wing.

8 With the top side up, fold the tip of the body down along the dotted line.

ATTACHING THE STRAW

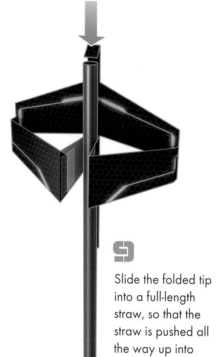

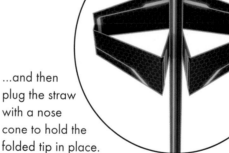

If you want a plane that flies far and fast, be slow and careful when you build it.

9

Slide the folded tip into a full-length straw, so that the straw is pushed all the way up into the crease...

...and then plug the straw with a nose cone to hold the folded tip in place.

10

Flip the jet over and line it up straight along the straw. Wrap a small piece of tape over the straw to hold the unattached end of the body in place.

Careful — if the plane is crooked on the straw, it won't fly straight.

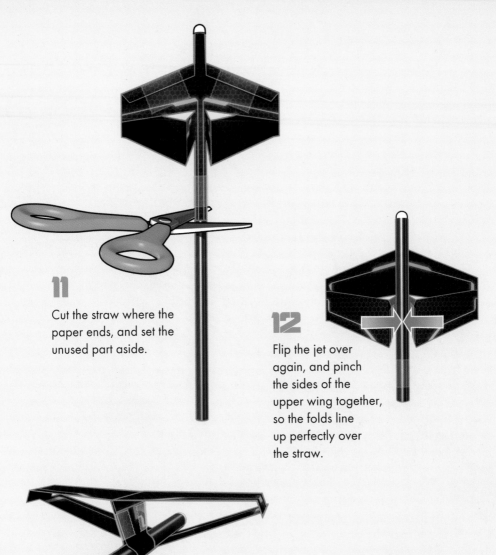

11

Cut the straw where the paper ends, and set the unused part aside.

12

Flip the jet over again, and pinch the sides of the upper wing together, so the folds line up perfectly over the straw.

13

Wrap a narrow strip of tape around the front and back edges of the vertical strut to hold the sides together...

...so it looks like this.

FLIGHT CHECK

Make sure all the folds are straight and line up with the straw. If they don't, fix them.

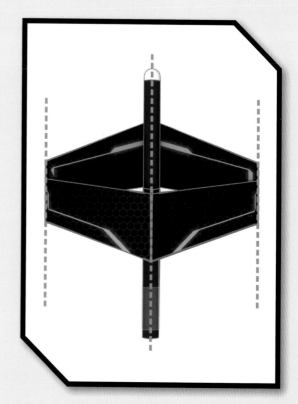

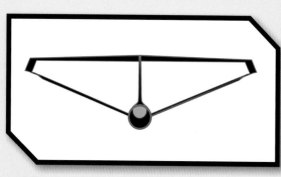

BALANCE

Look at your jet from the back. The wings should be symmetrical (looking the same on both sides). Does your jet match this picture? If not, adjust it.

READY FOR A TEST FLIGHT!

X·88

REAL AIRCRAFT INSPIRATION

BURGESS-DUNNE FLYING WING

There's no full-size aircraft that exactly matches the X-88. But the Burgess-Dunne Flying Wing series, built in the 1910s, shared some of the same features. It had box wings, it was the first flying wing design, and it was the first plane to fly without a tail. Unlike the X-88's tandem wings, the Burgess-Dunne's wings were stacked, making it a "biplane."

SPITFIRE

SPEED

RANGE

AGILITY

CONTROL

STYLE

When it comes to stunts, the dart-shaped Spitfire reigns supreme. Its delta-wing design produces very little drag, giving this jet great maneuverability at high speeds. Its vertical tail makes it easy to control. Plus, it boasts a longer range — though less combat skill — than its chief rival, the Strawhawk.

DELTA WING

VERTICAL TAIL

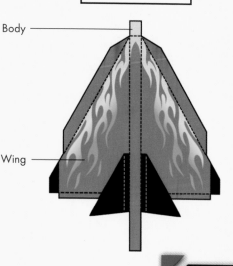

Body

Wing

Be sure to make
the detailed cuts.

CUT OUT THE SPITFIRE
For cutting tips, see page 7

FOLDING

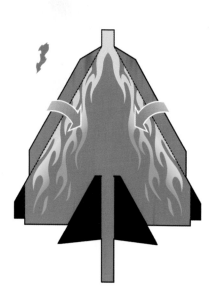

With the underside facing up,
fold along the dotted line at
the edge of each wing.

Stick a piece of tape on each wing
to hold the folds in place. Match
the size and placement of the tape
pieces as closely as you can.

Flip the plane top side up and fold both the wing tips in along the dotted lines. Then unfold.

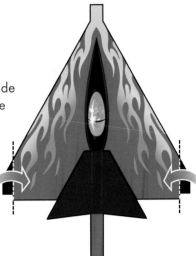

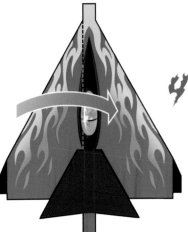

 Fold the left wing in. Crease, and then unfold.

Fold the wing only — not the tail.

Make each fold crisp and accurate. Take your time, hotshot. You're not in a race... yet.

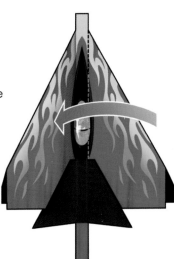 Do the same thing with the right wing — fold, crease, and unfold.

6 Fold the left tail fin in along the dotted line.

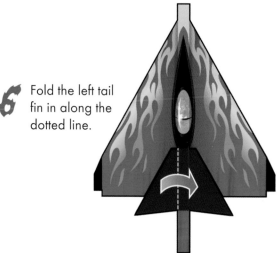

7 Fold the same tail fin back along the dotted line that is printed on the underside.

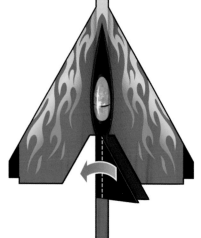

8

Repeat steps 6 and 7 with the right tail fin...

...and back along the underside dotted line.

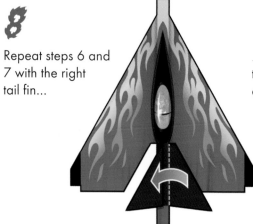

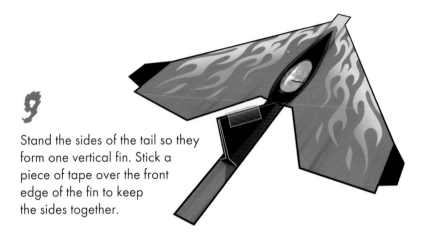

9
Stand the sides of the tail so they form one vertical fin. Stick a piece of tape over the front edge of the fin to keep the sides together.

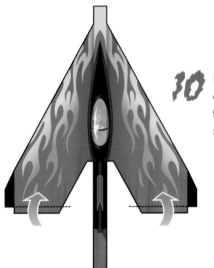

 10
Fold the tiny flap on each wing up along the dotted line. Crease and then unfold so these flaps are at a slight upward angle.

11
Flip the plane underside up. Fold the tip of the body along the dotted line.

ATTACHING THE STRAW

12 Slide the folded tip into a full-length straw, so that the straw is pushed all the way up into the crease...

...then plug the straw with a nose cone to hold the folded tip in place.

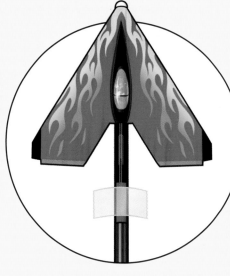

13

Flip the jet over and line it up so it is straight on the straw. Wrap a small piece of tape over the straw to hold the unattached end in place.

Careful — if the plane is crooked on the straw, it won't fly straight.

14 Cut the straw where the paper ends and set the unused part aside.

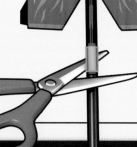

FLIGHT CHECK

Make sure the elevator flaps are at a slight upward angle, and all the other folds are straight and line up with the straw. If they don't, fix them.

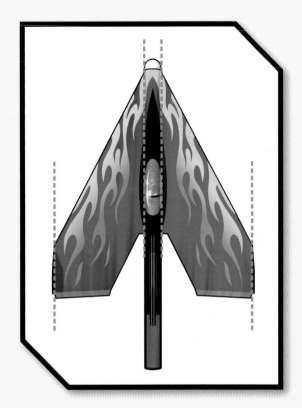

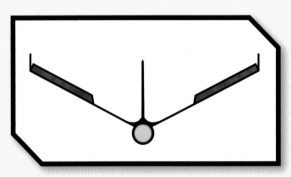

BALANCE

Look at your jet from the back. The wings should be symmetrical, and form a shallow V shape. The wing fins should be vertical. Does your jet match this picture? If not, adjust it.

READY FOR A TEST FLIGHT!

SPITFIRE
REAL AIRCRAFT INSPIRATION

EUROFIGHTER TYPHOON

Most real-life jets need horizontal flaps on the tail fin. But the Spitfire has a vertical tail with no horizontal surface. To do the same job as horizontal tail flaps, the Spitfire's wings sweep all the way back and line up with the tail. The Eurofighter Typhoon was designed the same way. It flies for the air forces of Germany, Spain, Italy, the United Kingdom, and Saudi Arabia, to name just a few.

Once you've mastered flying for distance, it's time to try a few...

STUNTS

You can experiment with all the jets, but the SPITFIRE is the best at stunts.

For each stunt, adjust the flaps as shown. Keep the angle of the wings symmetrical (the same on both sides) and rotate the jet on the straw to match the diagram.

BANK TURN

To do a right turn, angle the RIGHT flap UP, and flatten the left flap. To do a left turn, angle the LEFT flap UP, and flatten the right flap. Perfect for flying around corners.

VERTICAL LOOP

Fold your flaps so they are almost — but not entirely — straight up. With the wings level, shoot your jet at a dramatic upward angle as shown. For added flair, try to get your plane to fly over your head. Then turn around and catch it as it flies toward you.

THE BOOMERANG

Fold your flaps so they are almost — but not entirely — straight up. Aim diagonally upward, then rotate your straw so that the wings are angled diagonally right or left. When you blow, the plane will bank around and fly right back toward you.

AILERON ROLL

Angle the RIGHT flap UP, and flatten the left flap. Rotate your straw to the RIGHT so the wings match the diagram. When you blow, the plane will roll over once clockwise and level out. To do a counterclockwise roll, just reverse these directions.

CORKSCREW

Set the two flaps opposite each other, with one angled up and one angled down. Aim your launch for a slightly higher angle than usual and blow hard. Instead of gliding, your plane will spin violently in the air. Shoot straight up for a daredevil corkscrew nosedive!

If your launches need a R.A.D. refresher, turn to page 12.

TROUBLESHOOTING

1. Find the problem from the list below. 2. Make one adjustment. 3. Launch the jet again.

PROBLEM

"My plane flies up steeply, then dives down."

SOLUTION

If your plane has flaps, flatten them.

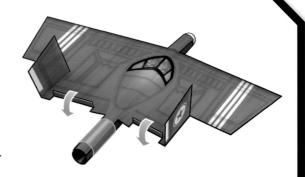

PROBLEM

"My plane dives straight for the ground."

SOLUTION

Aim your launch a little higher. If your plane has flaps, angle them up a little.

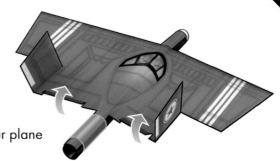

PROBLEM

"My plane doesn't go very far."

SOLUTION

Make sure your launch straw is pressed all the way up against the inside of the nosecone. The less space there is in the straw, the more compressed the air will be, and the better velocity and distance you'll get.

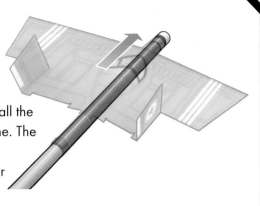

PROBLEM

"My plane keeps turning one way and I want it to go straight."

SOLUTION

Make sure your wings are pushed up to form a V shape and are symmetrical. If your plane has flaps, push up, just a little, on the flap of the wing that's opposite the direction of the turn.

DON'T DESPAIR, REPAIR

Crashes are inevitable. But a few crinkles and tears don't mean your jet's destined for the scrapyard. Use a small piece of tape — just big enough to cover the tear — to repair the damage.

If you add tape on one wing, balance it with another piece on the other wing.

EXPAND

★★★ YOUR FLEET ★★★

Repairing your jet with tape can only do so much. At some point it will be too wrinkled and weighed down to fly. But don't throw away the whole thing! All you have to do is replace the paper. Here's how you save the rest of the plane.

NOSE CONES

Pull the nose cone out of the jet straw.

THE JET STRAW

Carefully remove the tape holding the rear of the plane to the jet straw.

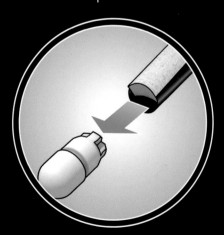

Finding Replacement Straws

We've provided you with more paper planes than jet straws. You can always replace the jet straws with any plastic drinking straw that the nose cones can plug into and that the shooting straw can slip inside freely.

STENCIL

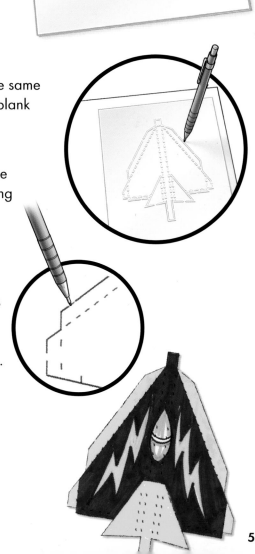

In the back of the book is a stencil of the Spitfire design. With this tool, you can turn other sheets of paper into flight-ready jets.

1 Find a sheet of paper that's about the same thickness as the Fleet Sheets. (Either blank or patterned — it's up to you.)

2 Place the stencil over the paper so the outline of the jet fits on the sheet. Using a mechanical pencil or fine-tip pen, trace the entire stencil. Then set the stencil aside.

3 Note that some of the outer solid lines aren't connected. Connect them. Don't connect the dashed lines — those show you where to make a fold.

4 Add color, design details, and, of course, a cockpit. When you are done designing, follow the instructions for cutting, folding, and taping the Spitfire (pages 42 – 48).

MEET THE FLEETS

	DRAGONFLY	STRAWHAWK
SKY PIRATES		
SPIT-WADS		
AIR FORCE		
STEALTH		
HOT SHOTS	 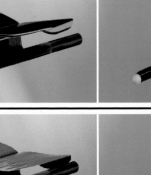	 

Each of the five Straw Shooter Jet designs comes in five different teams, or "fleets." For a sneak peek at all of the fleets, look below. Or just look on the real Fleet Sheets. They start just around the corner, beyond the next page.

| VIPER | X-88 | SPITFIRE |

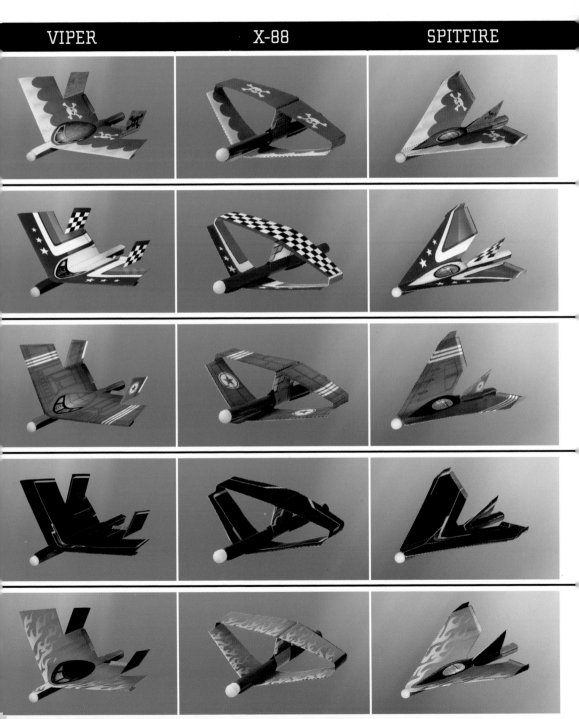

CREDITS

Big Shot (Concept, Aircraft Design and Illustration): Quillon Tsang

Art Director: Michael Sherman

Designer: Kevin Plottner

Editor: Karen Phillips

Editorial Assistant and P. Shooter Illustrator: Dan Letchworth

Tech Artist: Steve Kongsle

Package Designer: David Avidor

Production Editor: Madeleine Robins

Buyer/Planner: Mimi Oey

Quality Assurance: Karen Fuchs, Meryl Wolfe

Photographer: Rory Earnshaw

Model: Nolan Jessen

Photo Researcher: Amia Sanghvi

Special Thanks: Paul Doherty, Barb Magnus, Jill Turney, and Pat Murphy

Here are more Klutz books we think your kids will like.

THE FLEET SHEETS

DRAGONFLY

BUILDING INSTRUCTIONS ON PAGE 14

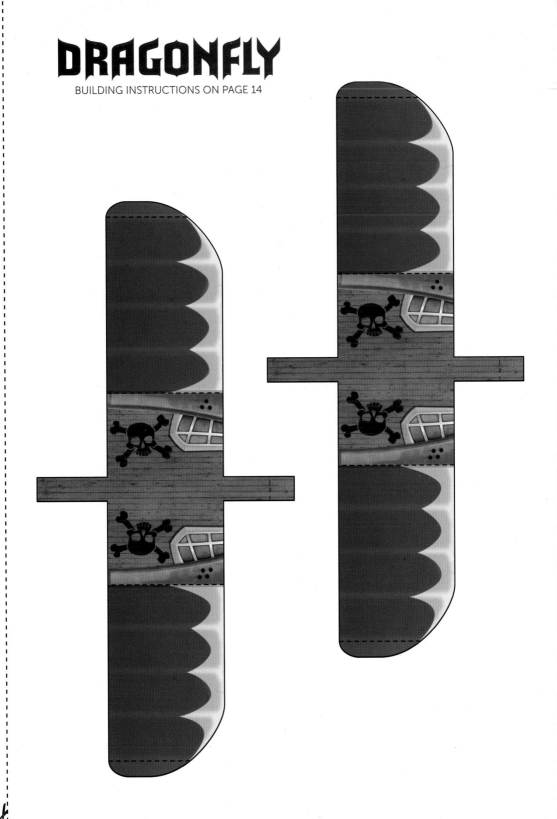

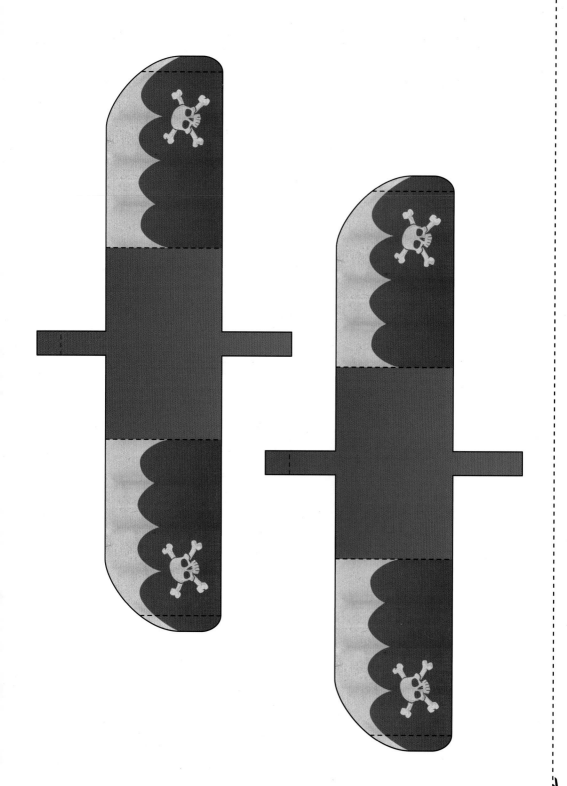

DRAGONFLY

BUILDING INSTRUCTIONS ON PAGE 14

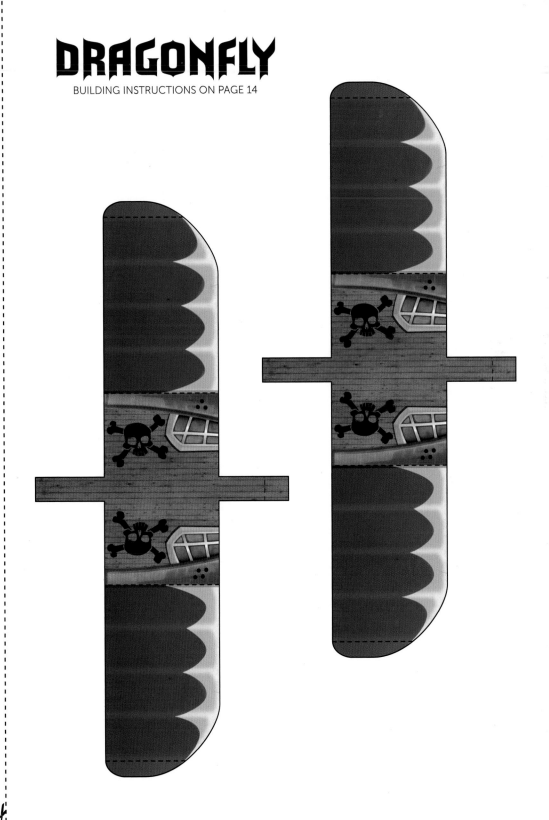

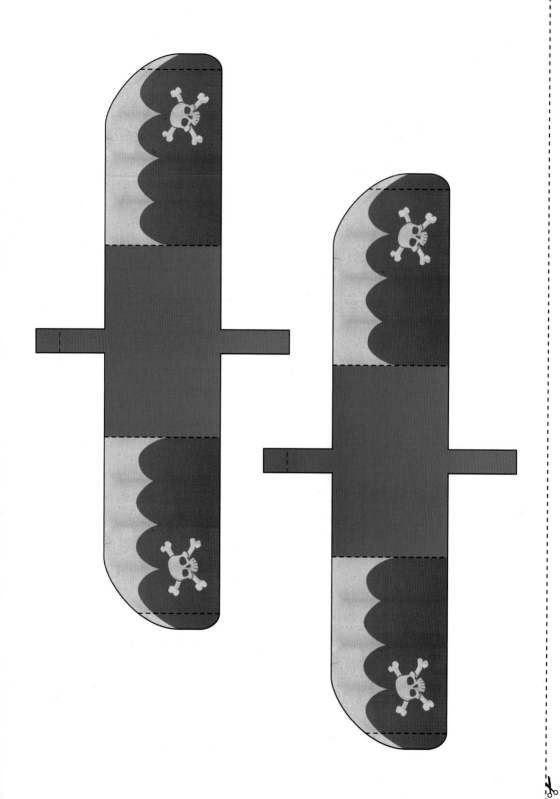

DRAGONFLY

BUILDING INSTRUCTIONS ON PAGE 14

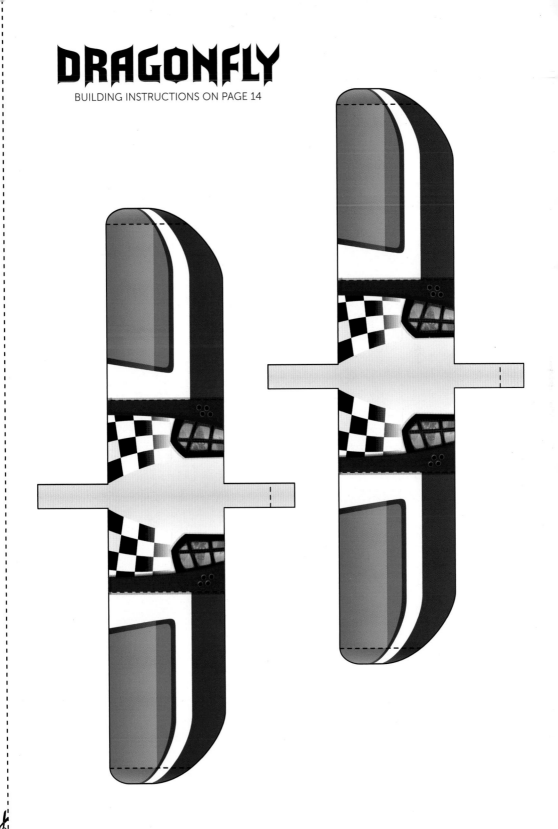

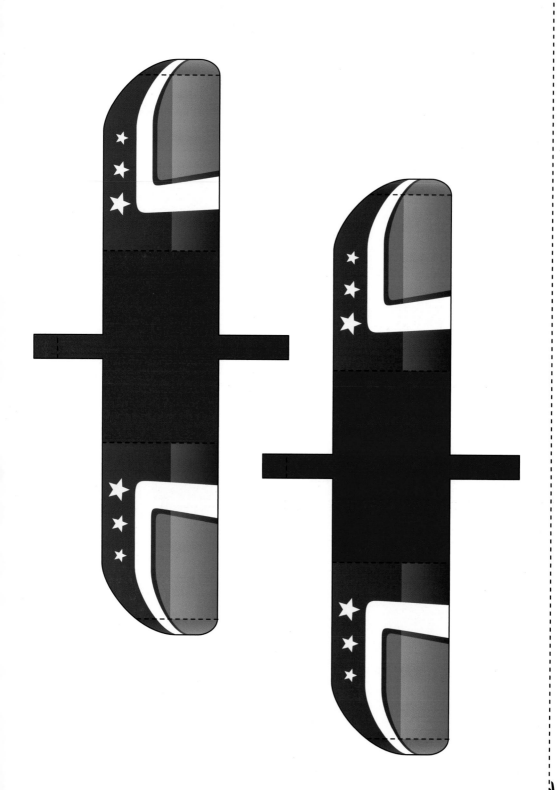

DRAGONFLY

BUILDING INSTRUCTIONS ON PAGE 14

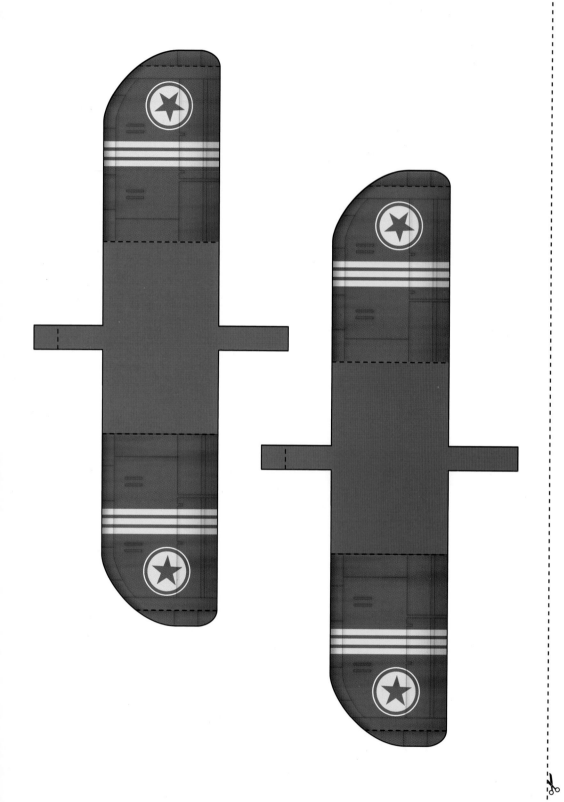

DRAGONFLY

BUILDING INSTRUCTIONS ON PAGE 14

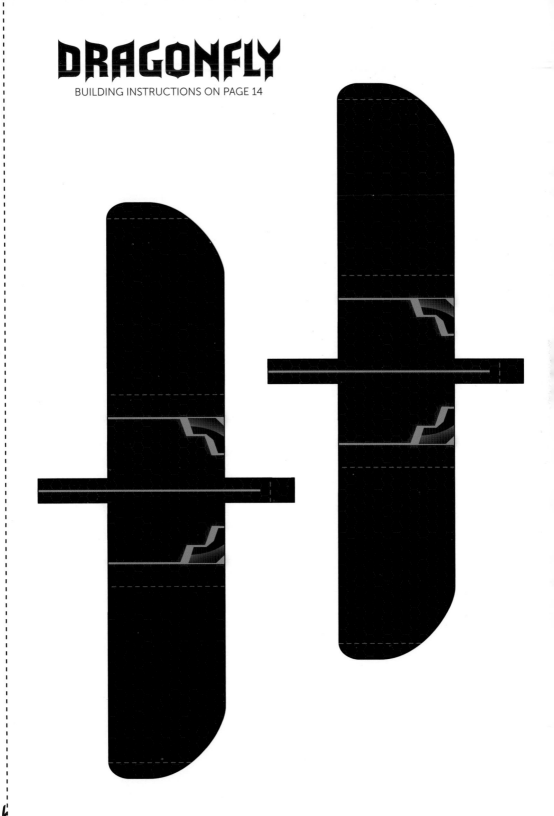

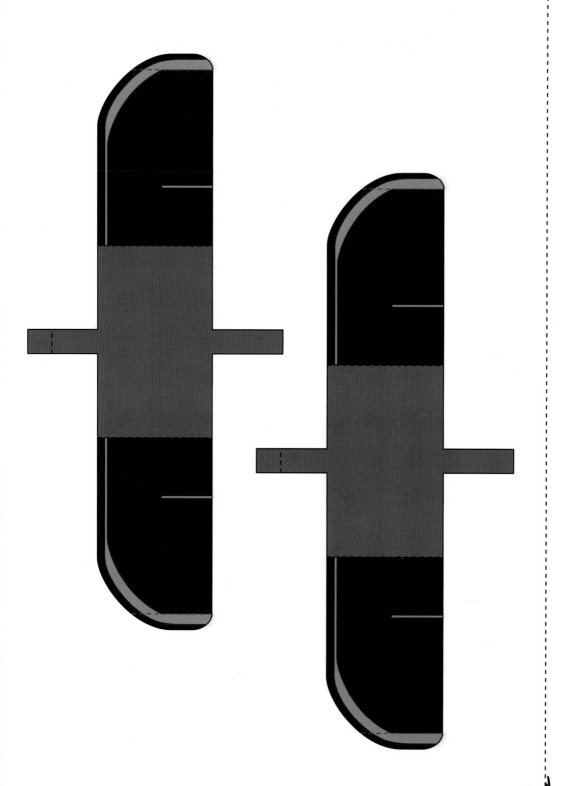

DRAGONFLY

BUILDING INSTRUCTIONS ON PAGE 14

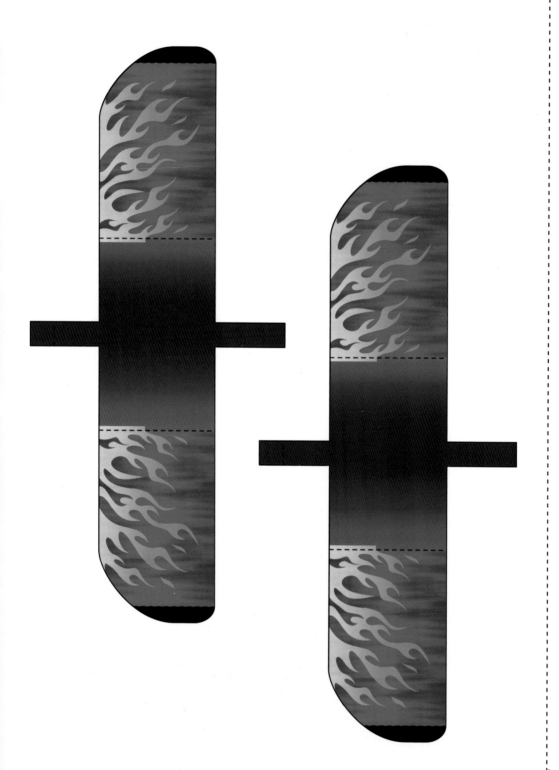

STRAWHAWK

BUILDING INSTRUCTIONS ON PAGE 20

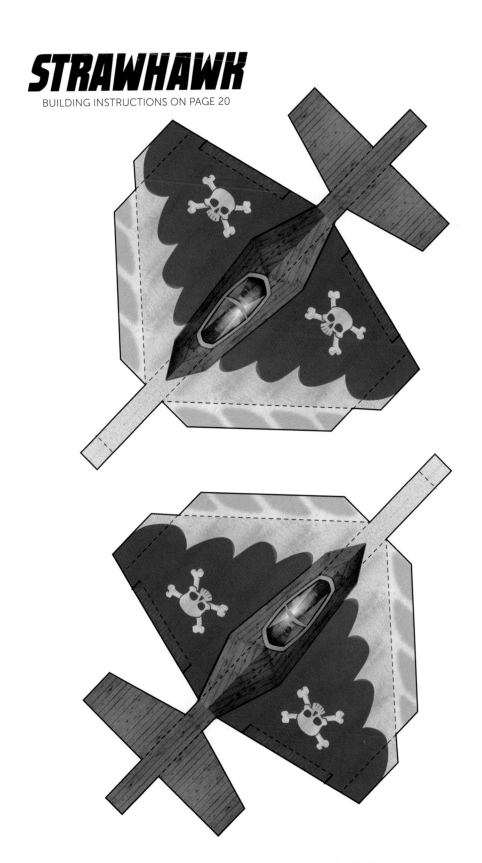

STRAWHAWK

BUILDING INSTRUCTIONS ON PAGE 20

STRAWHAWK

BUILDING INSTRUCTIONS ON PAGE 20

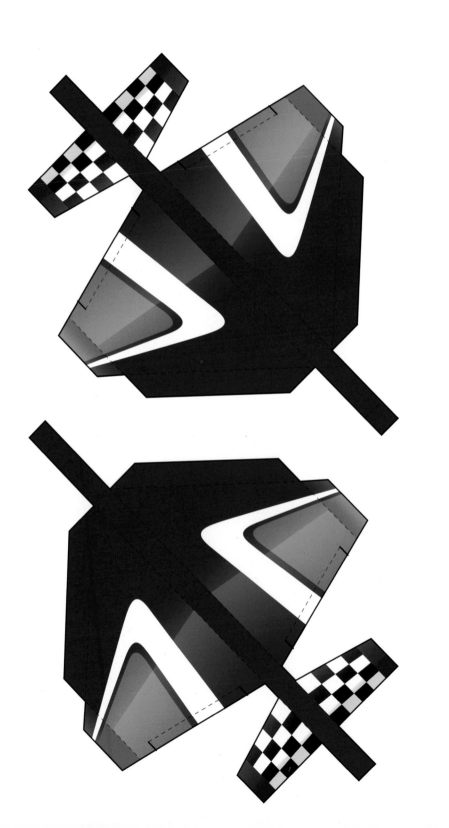

STRAWHAWK

BUILDING INSTRUCTIONS ON PAGE 20

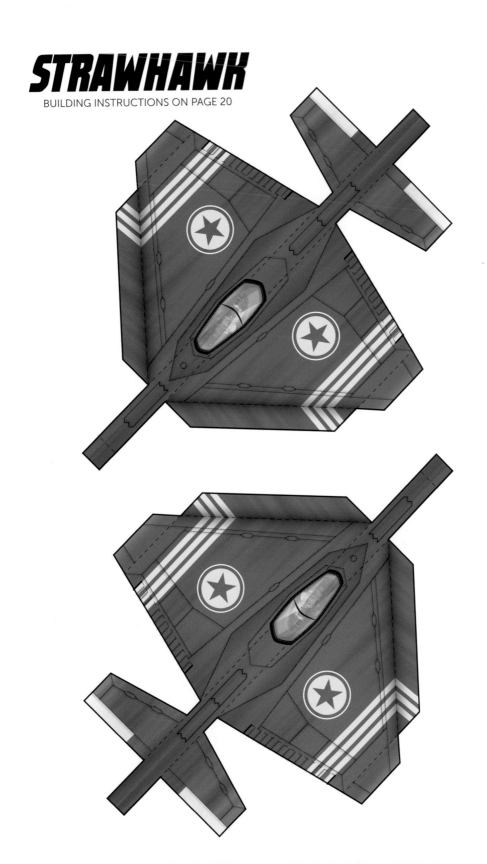

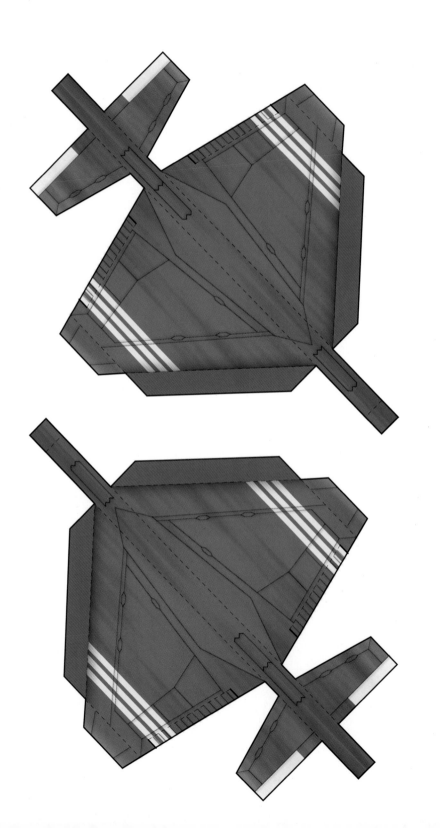

STRAWHAWK

BUILDING INSTRUCTIONS ON PAGE 20

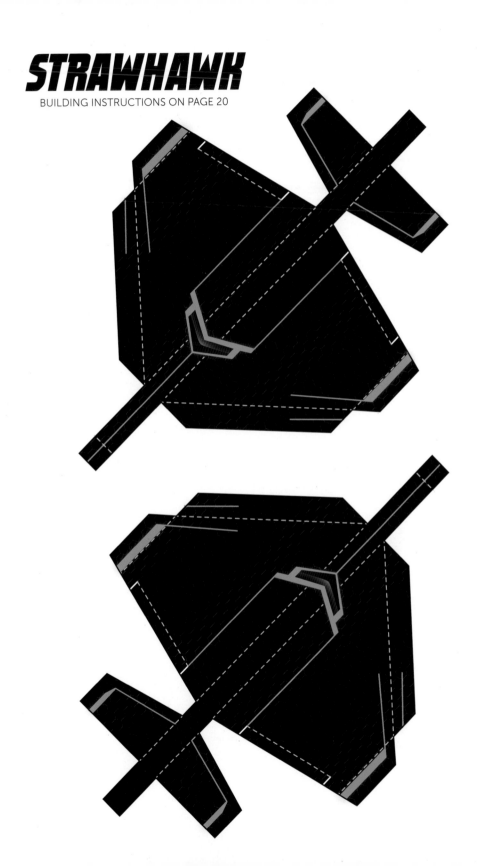

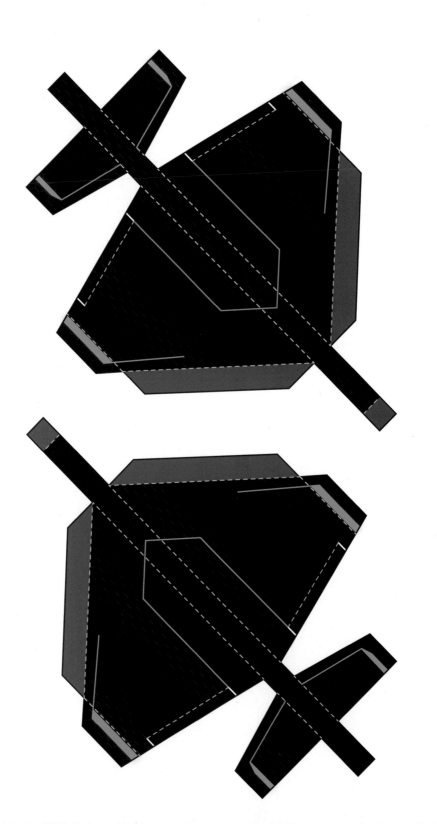

STRAWHAWK

BUILDING INSTRUCTIONS ON PAGE 20

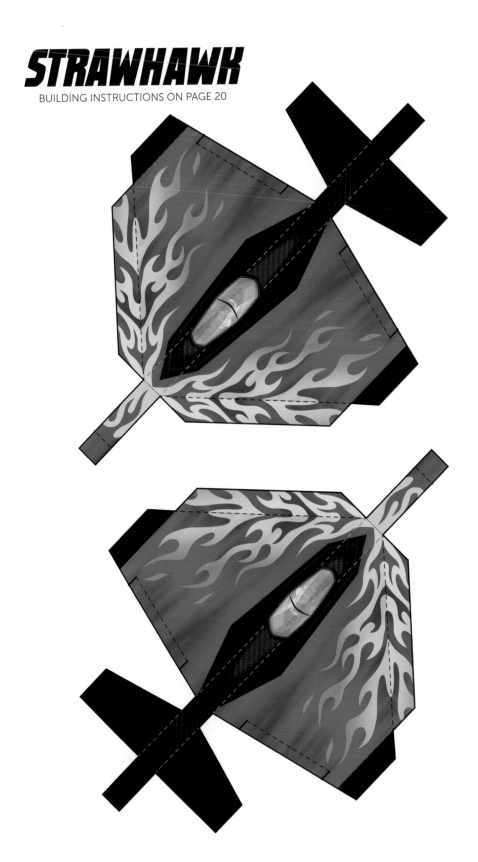

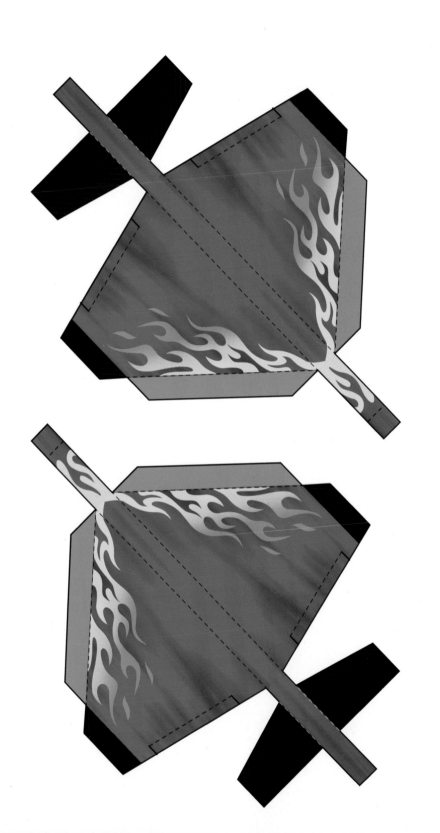

VIPER

BUILDING INSTRUCTIONS ON PAGE 26

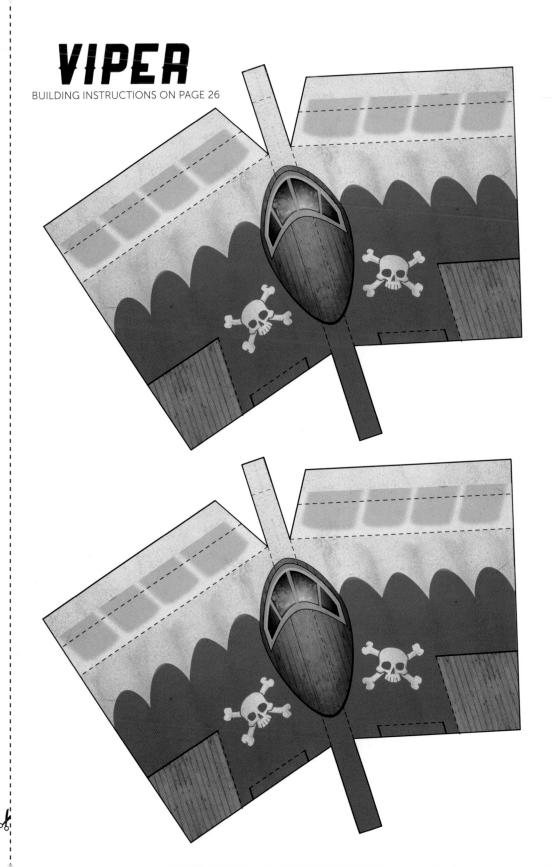

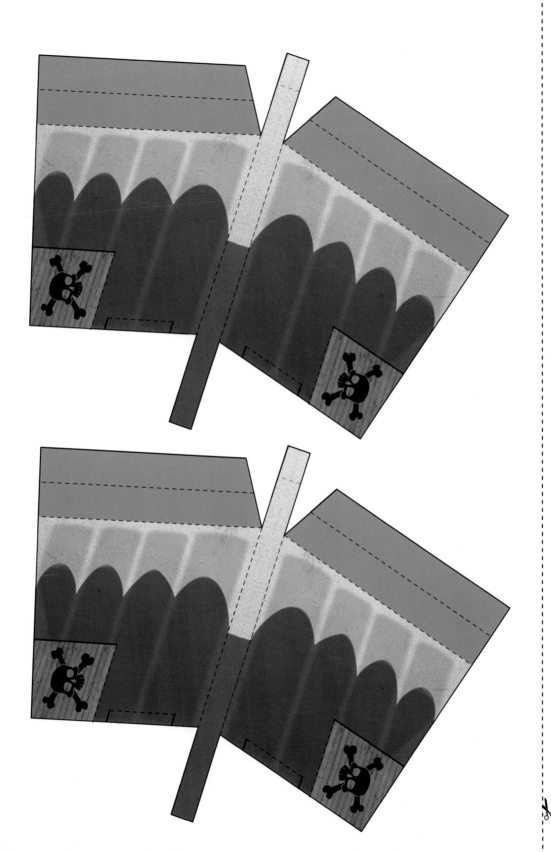

VIPER

BUILDING INSTRUCTIONS ON PAGE 26

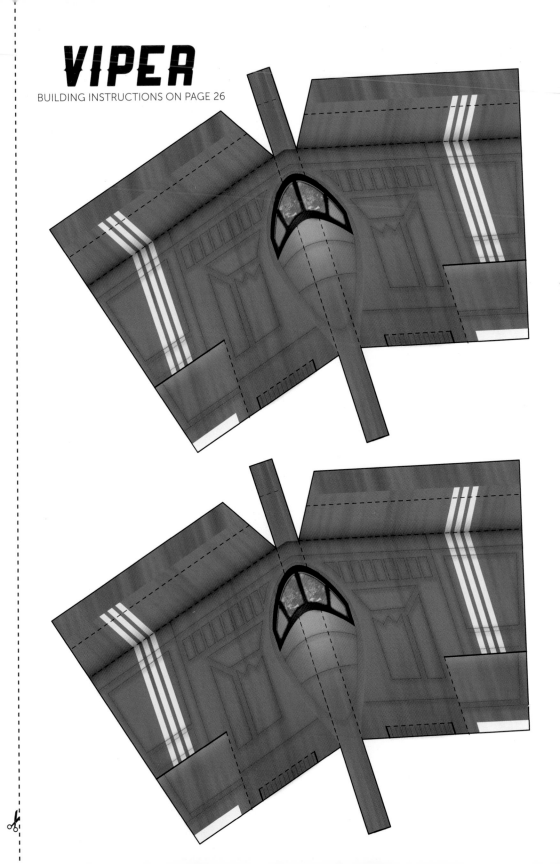

VIPER
BUILDING INSTRUCTIONS ON PAGE 26

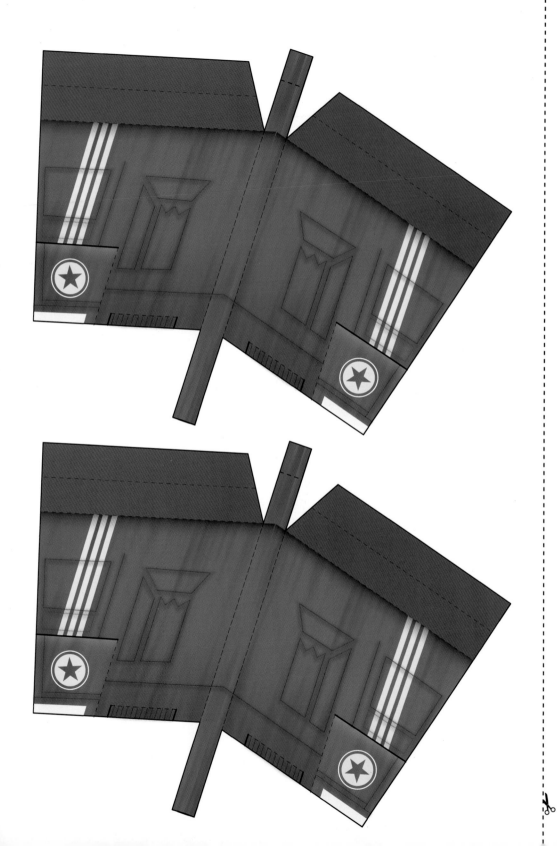

VIPER

BUILDING INSTRUCTIONS ON PAGE 26

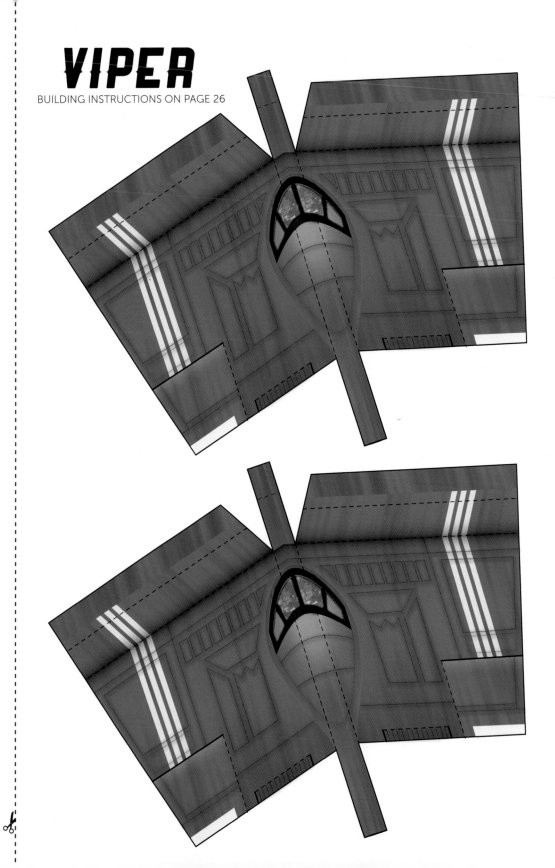

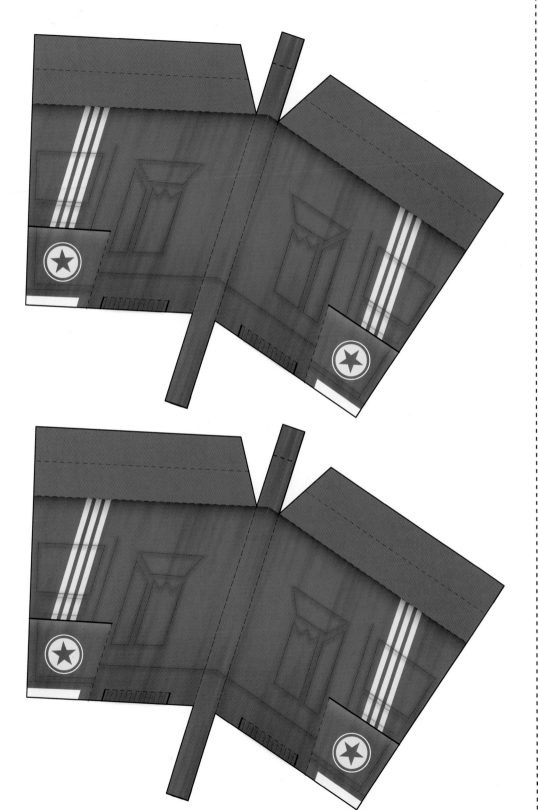

VIPER

BUILDING INSTRUCTIONS ON PAGE 26

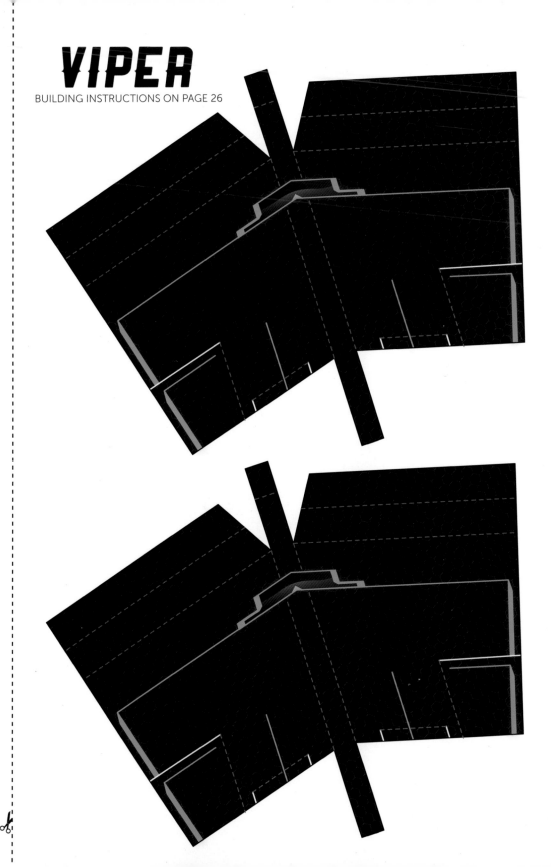

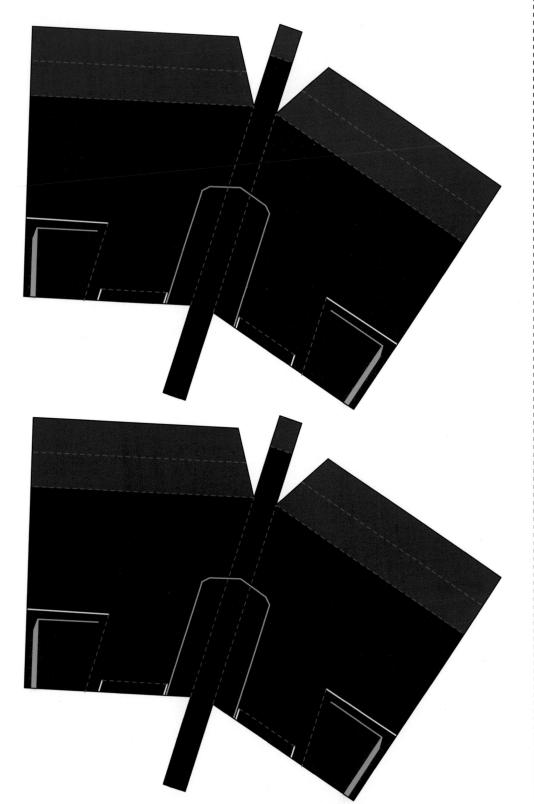

VIPER

BUILDING INSTRUCTIONS ON PAGE 26

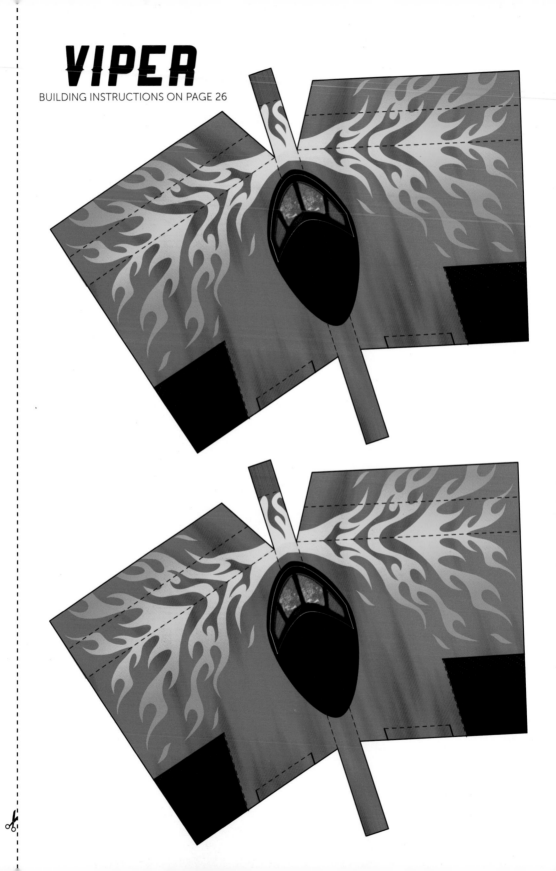

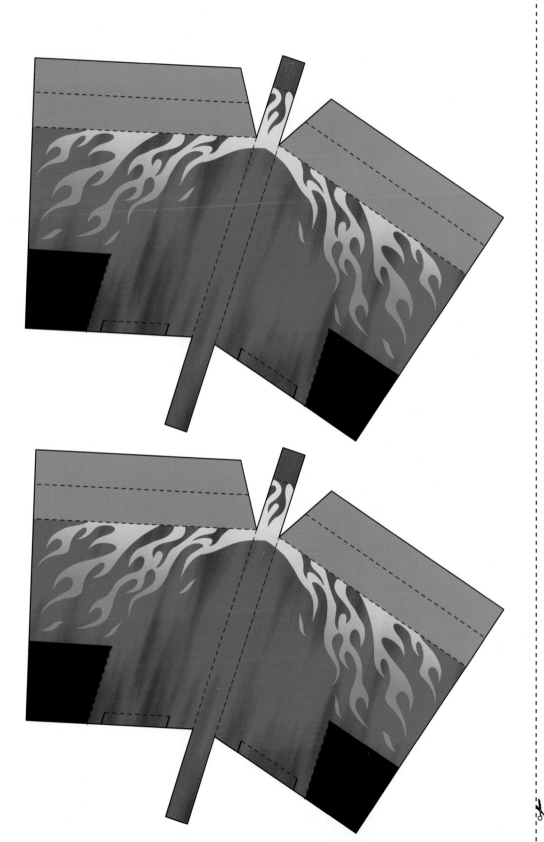

X·88

BUILDING INSTRUCTIONS ON PAGE 34

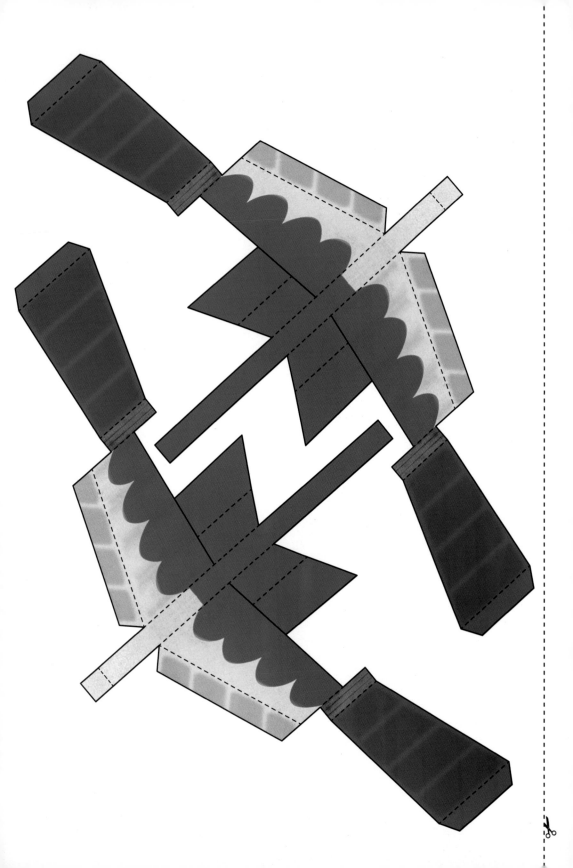

X-88

BUILDING INSTRUCTIONS ON PAGE 34

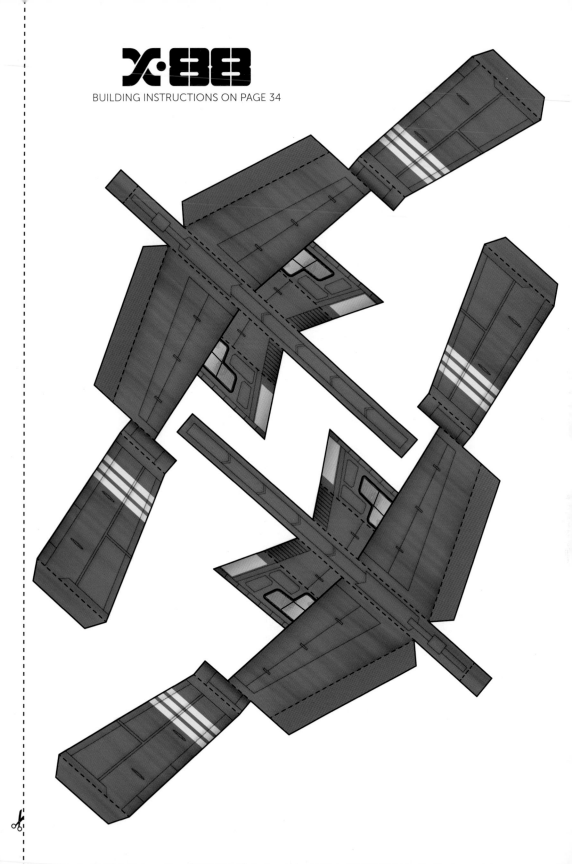

X·88
BUILDING INSTRUCTIONS ON PAGE 34

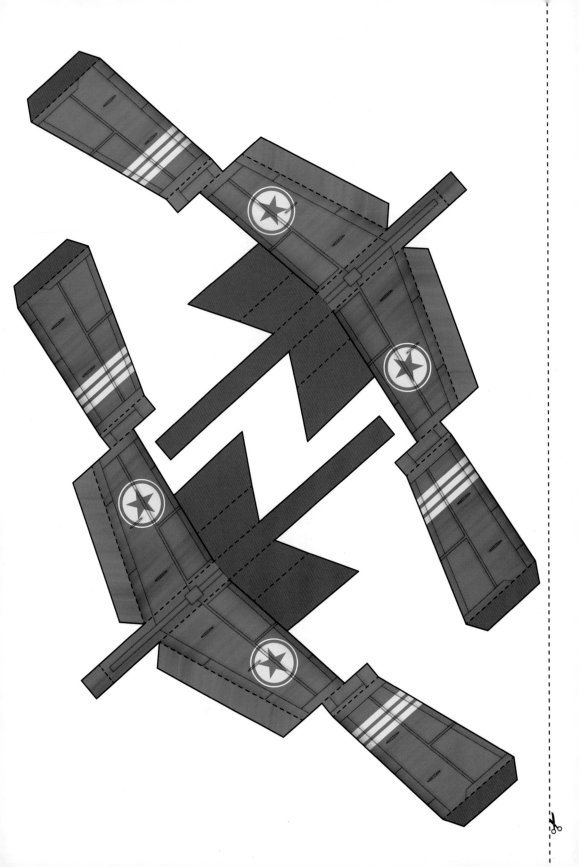

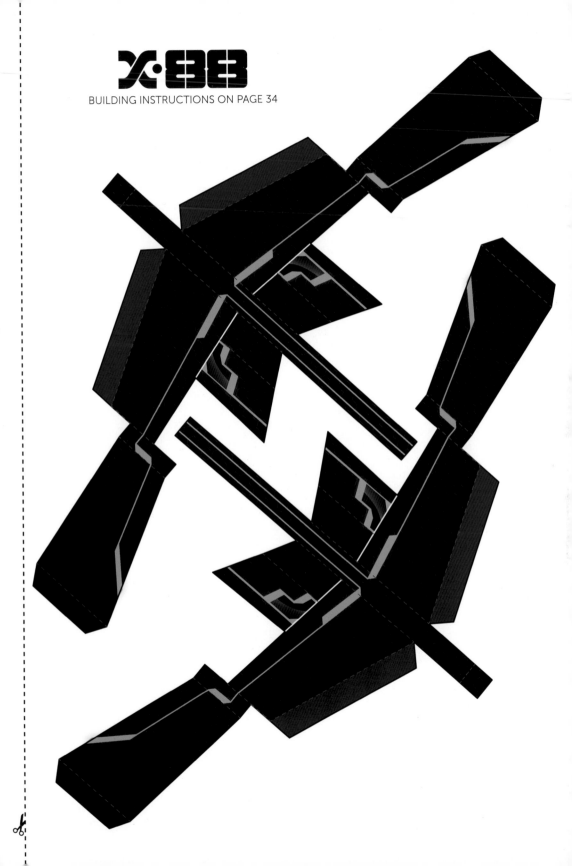

X·88

BUILDING INSTRUCTIONS ON PAGE 34

X-88

BUILDING INSTRUCTIONS ON PAGE 34

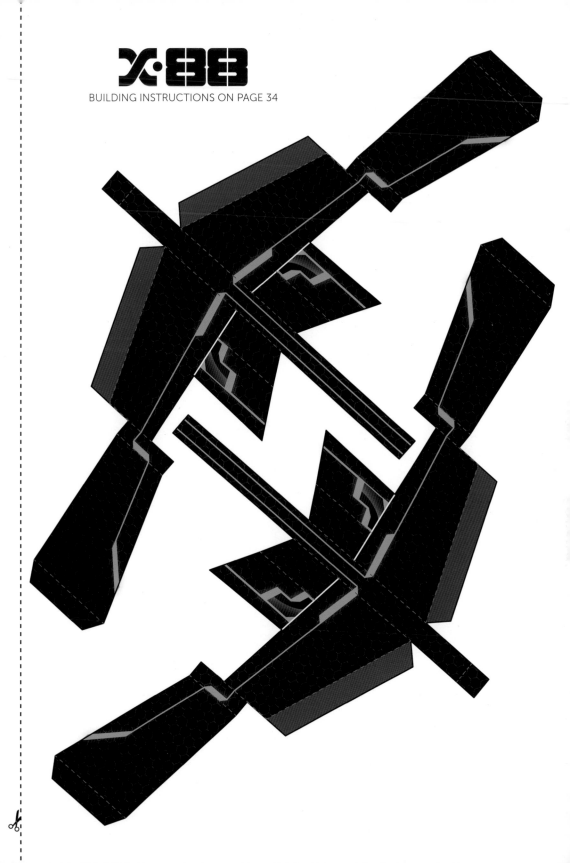

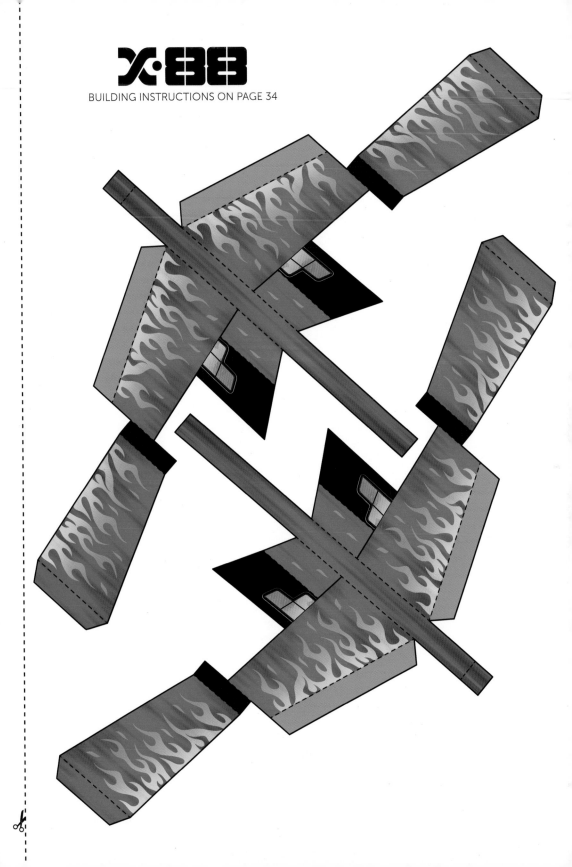

X·88

BUILDING INSTRUCTIONS ON PAGE 34

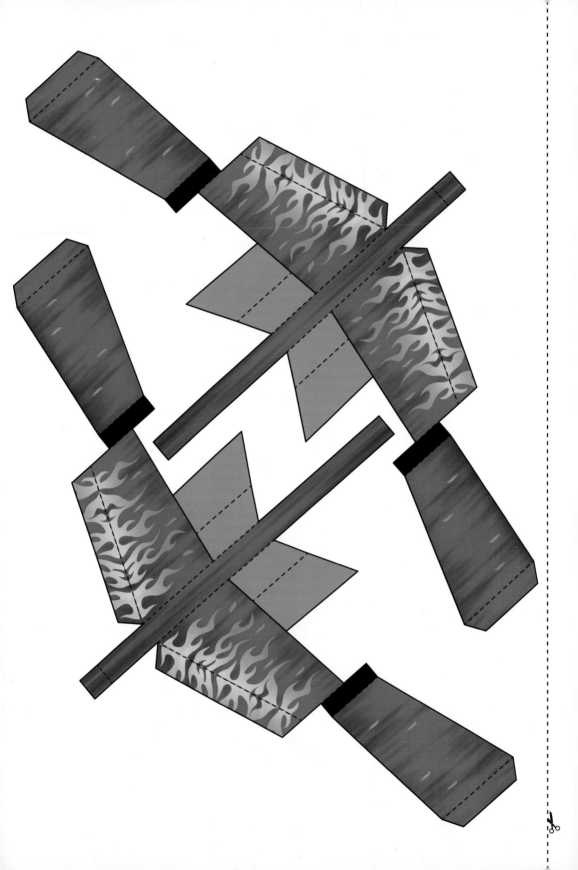

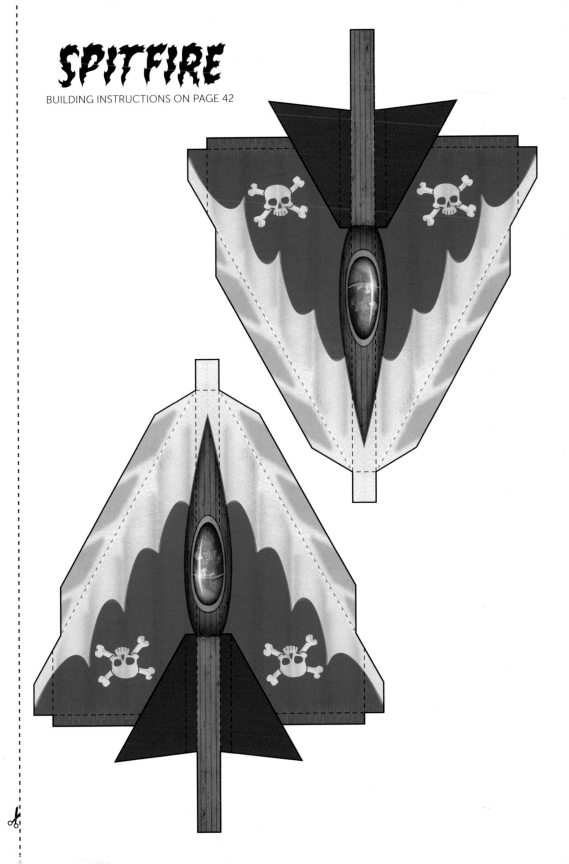

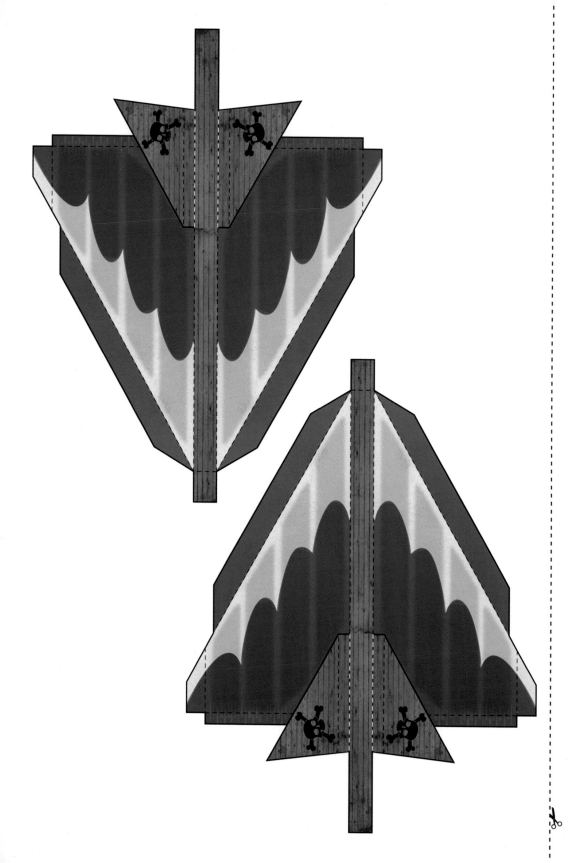

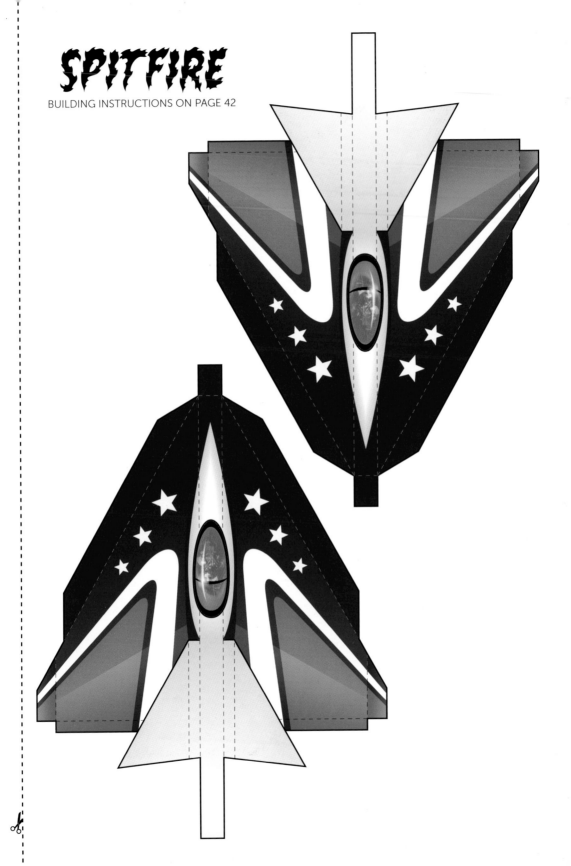

SPITFIRE

BUILDING INSTRUCTIONS ON PAGE 42

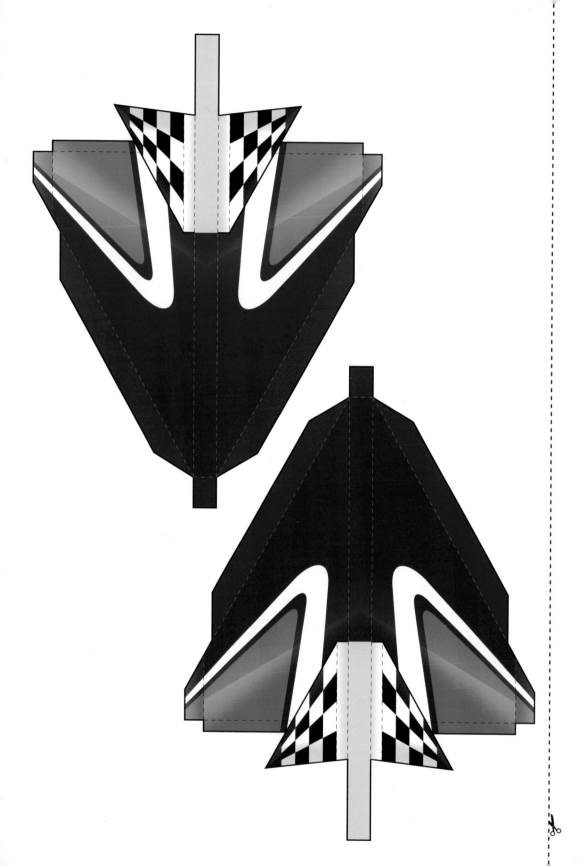

SPITFIRE

BUILDING INSTRUCTIONS ON PAGE 42

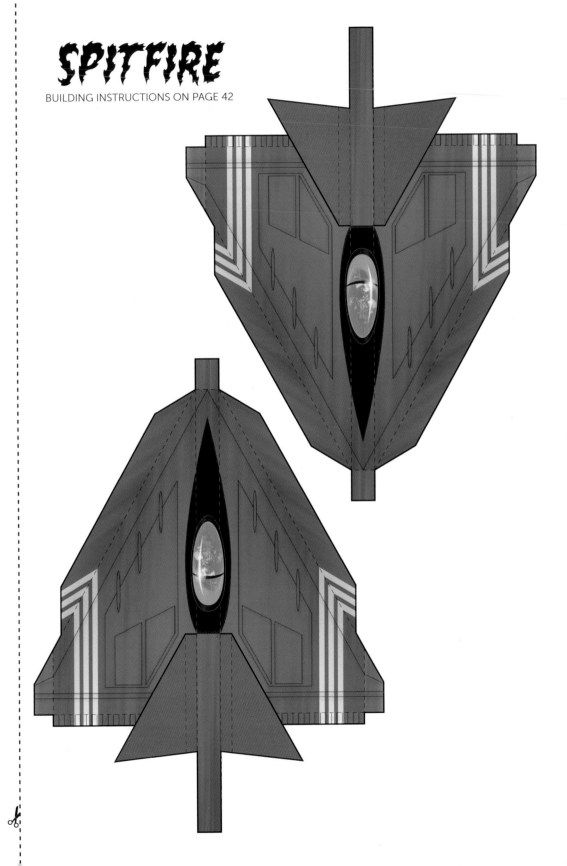

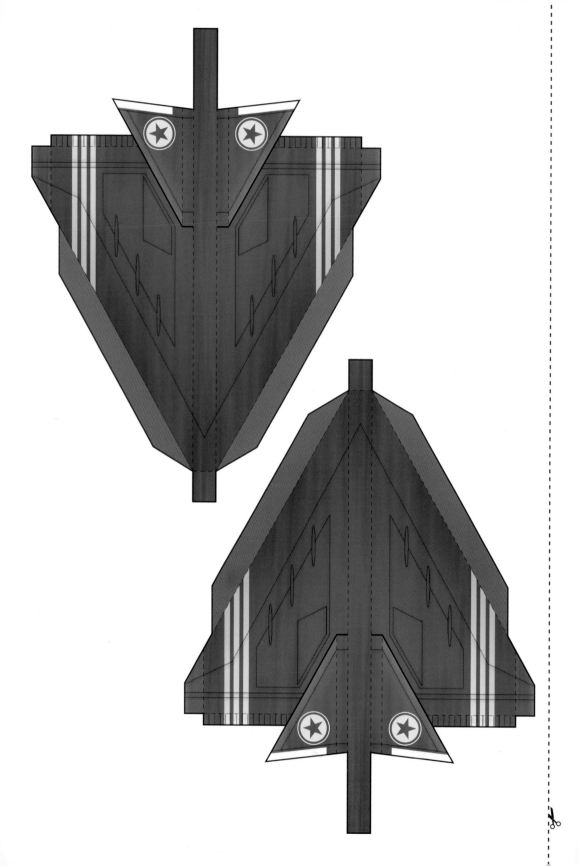

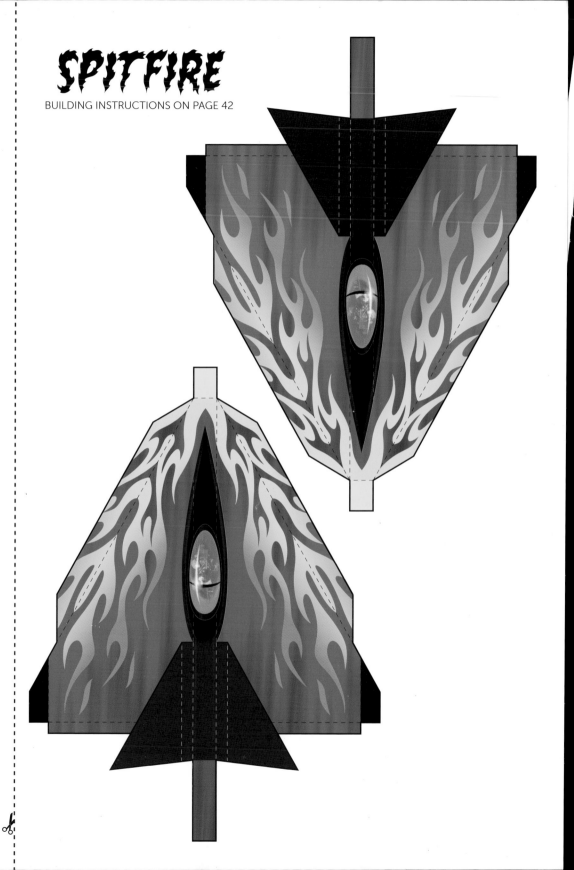

SPITFIRE

BUILDING INSTRUCTIONS ON PAGE 42

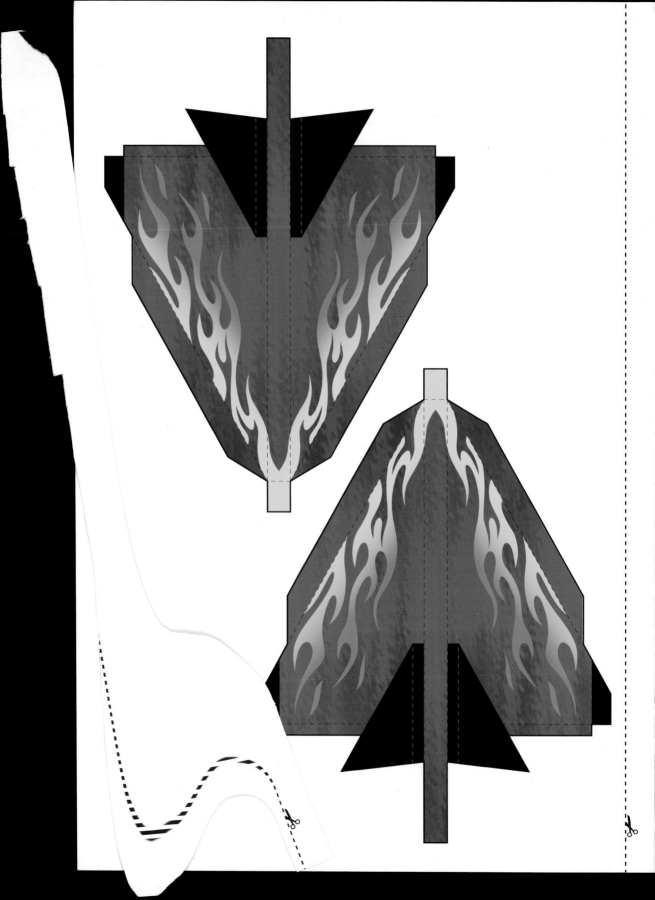

SPITFIRE

BUILDING INSTRUCTIONS ON PAGE 42

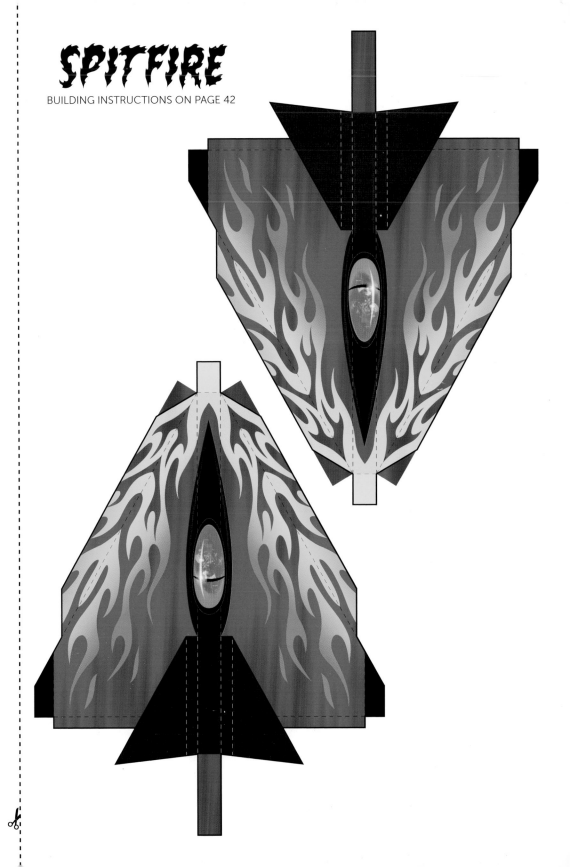

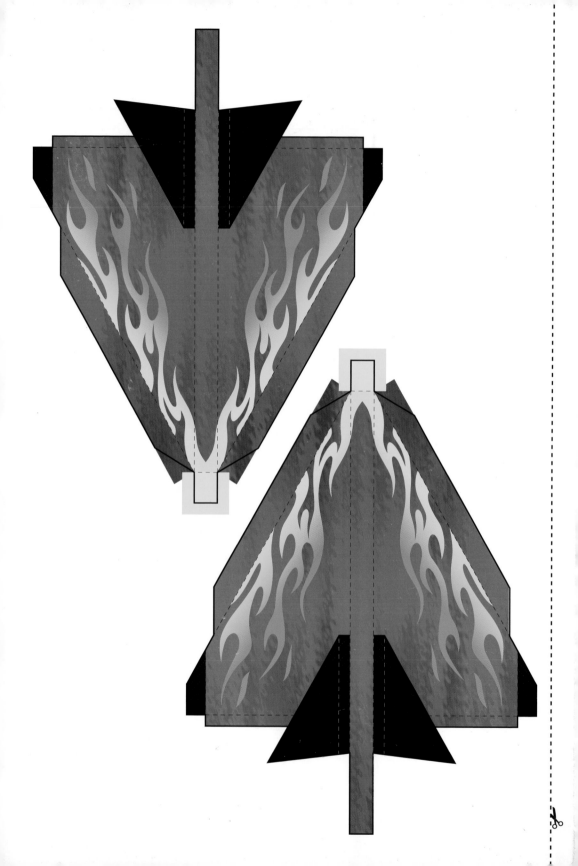